The Teachings of Jesus and Muhammad

The Teachings of Jesus and Muhammad

MATEEN ELASS

Published by eChristian, Inc.
Escondido, California

The Teachings of Jesus and Muhammad

Copyright © 2013 by Mateen Elass. All rights reserved.

First printing in 2013 by eChristian, Inc.
eChristian, Inc.
2235 Enterprise Street, Suite 140
Escondido, CA 92029
http://echristian.com

ISBN: 978-1-61843-310-7

Scripture marked (NIV) are taken from THE HOLY BIBLE, NEW INTERNATIONAL VERSION®, NIV® Copyright © 1973, 1978, 1984, 2011 by Biblica, Inc.™ Used by permission. All rights reserved worldwide.

Scripture marked (NLT) are taken from the *Holy Bible*, New Living Translation, copyright © 1996, 2004, 2007 by Tyndale House Foundation. Used by permission of Tyndale House Publishers, Inc., Carol Stream, Illinois 60188. All rights reserved.

Scripture marked (ESV) are from The Holy Bible, English Standard Version, copyright © 2001 by Crossway Bibles, a division of Good News Publishers. Used by permission. All rights reserved.

Scripture marked (NKJV) taken from the *New King James Version*. Copyright © 1979, 1980, 1982 by Thomas Nelson, Inc. Used by permission. All rights reserved.

Quran verses taken from The Noble Quran, translated into the modern English Language by Dr. Muhammad Taqi-ud-Din Al-Hilali, Ph.D. & Dr. Muhammad Muhsin Khan (http://www.dar-us-salam.com/TheNobleQuran/index.html). Published by Dar-us-Salam Publications.

Cover and interior design by Larry Taylor.

Produced with the assistance of Livingstone, the Publishing Services Division of eChristian, Inc. Project staff includes: Bruce Barton, Dan Balow, Afton Rorvik, Linda Washington, Linda Taylor, Claudia Gerwin, Ashley Taylor, Lois Jackson, Andy Culbertson, and Tom Shumaker.

Printed in the United States of America

19 18 17 16 15 14 13 12 8 7 6 5 4 3 2 1

Table of Contents

Introduction

When it comes to the most powerful influencers on the thoughts and actions of the entire human race today, two figures tower above all other contenders: Jesus and Muhammad. Over half the world's population openly claims to follow the teachings and commands of one of these two leaders. Many of the rest have grown up in cultures whose present mores and values find their roots in the rich soil of the Bible or Quran. Though such individuals may carry no personal allegiance to either Jesus or Muhammad, their psyches and dreams have nonetheless been shaped by the movements launched by the lives of one of these two.

Yet Jesus and Muhammad present two different, often contrasting, sometimes contradictory, visions of the meaning and purpose of life. In one sense, this should not be surprising. Muhammad lived six centuries after Jesus, grew up in a pagan versus monotheistic environment, was unfamiliar with the Bible (since there was no Arabic translation and Muhammad knew no other languages) but steeped in Arab folklore. On the other hand, both Muhammad and Jesus made clear pronouncements about many of the same spiritual, theological, and moral issues common to the Semitic peoples.

This book seeks to set the teachings of Jesus and Muhammad side by side on sixty themes, posed in the form of questions, so that the reader may compare and contrast them. The "Perspective" section is offered to stimulate further thought on the teachings and claims of these two seminal leaders.

One need not be a prophet to envision that the coming decades will see increasing interplay between Christians and Muslims in the West. Perhaps this book will play a small part in shedding light where there is often all too much ignorance.

Special thanks are due to Bruce Barton and his staff at Livingstone for seeing this project to fruition, as well as to eChristian for their willingness to publish this material. As always, any errors of content or unfounded bias are strictly my own.

—Mateen Elass
December 6, 2012

1. Is God the Father of Jesus?

The Bible says:

John 5:17–18 (NLT)

But Jesus replied, "My Father is always working, and so am I." So the Jewish leaders tried all the harder to find a way to kill him. For he not only broke the Sabbath, he called God his Father, thereby making himself equal with God.

John 10:25–30 (NLT)

Jesus replied, "I have already told you, and you don't believe me. The proof is the work I do in my Father's name. But you don't believe me because you are not my sheep. My sheep listen to my voice; I know them, and they follow me. I give them eternal life, and they will never perish. No one can snatch them away from me, for my Father has given them to me, and he is more powerful than anyone else. No one can snatch them from the Father's hand. The Father and I are one."

John 17:1, 4–5 (NLT)

After saying all these things, Jesus looked up to heaven and said, "Father, the hour has come. Glorify your Son so he can give glory back to you. . . . I brought glory to you here on earth by completing the work you gave me to do. Now, Father, bring me into the glory we shared before the world began."

Matthew 11:27 (NLT)

My Father has entrusted everything to me. No one truly knows the Son except the Father, and no one truly knows the Father except the Son and those to whom the Son chooses to reveal him.

The Quran says:

112:1–4

Say (O Muhammad): "He is Allah, (the) One. *Allah-us-Samad* (The Self-Sufficient Master, Whom all creatures need, He neither eats nor drinks). He begets not, nor was He begotten; And there is none co-equal or comparable unto Him."

19:88–93

And they say: "The Most Beneficent (Allah) has begotten a son (or offspring or children) [as the Jews say: 'Uzair (Ezra) is the son of Allah, and the Christians say that He has begotten a son ['Isa (Christ)], and the pagan Arabs say that He has begotten daughters (angels, etc.)]." Indeed you have brought forth (said) a terrible evil thing. Whereby the heavens are almost torn, and the earth is split asunder, and the mountains fall in ruins, That they ascribe a son (or offspring or children) to the Most Beneficent (Allah). But it is not suitable for (the Majesty of) the Most Beneficent (Allah) that He should beget a son (or offspring or children). There is none in the heavens and the earth but comes unto the Most Beneficent (Allah) as a slave.

Perspective:

Jesus' disciple, John, in his Gospel, refers to Jesus several times as "the one and only Son" of the Father (John 1:14; 3:16ff.). Where did he get the idea that Jesus enjoyed a unique relationship with God in heaven that is unlike that of any other human being? The answer must be from Jesus Himself. No Jew would dare to claim such intimacy and equality with God, nor would an observant Jew be willing to ascribe such stature to another human being, unless of course he was convinced that such an individual was indeed more than merely human. Jesus' most frequent title for God was "my Father," and "Father" is the address Jesus invariably uses in His prayers to God (the lone exception to this is His quotation of Psalm 22:1 while in agony on the cross—Matthew 27:46). John emphasizes the enormity of Jesus' claim in speaking of God as His Father: "For this reason they tried all the more to kill him; not only was he breaking the Sabbath, but he was even calling God his own Father, making himself equal with God" (John 5:18). In John 10:25–30 Jesus again highlights His unique relationship with God as His Father, and goes so far as to say "I and the Father are one." As a result, those listening seek to stone Him for blasphemy because, they say, "You, a mere man, claim to be God" (10:33). That Jesus sees God as His Father in a unique way is confirmed by the fact that Jesus never speaks to others of God as "our Father." When the disciples ask Him how to pray, He teaches *them* to say together "Our Father" (Matthew 6:9), but when He has the perfect opportunity to lump Himself together with other human beings as sons and daughters in relationship to God, He avoids this by saying "to my Father and your Father" (John 20:17). As Matthew 11:27 demonstrates, Jesus sees Himself as the unique Son of God—only through Him can others come to God, because only Jesus can reveal the Father to the world.

Muhammad, on the other hand, believed that anyone who knowingly claimed to be "son of God" singled himself out as an evil person and enemy of God, because no human being could be anything other than a servant or slave of God. According to Sura 19:89, such a claim is "monstrous" or "hideous," so cataclysmic that it could cause the earth to be sundered and mountains to be uprooted. Likewise, Sura 112 condemns both polytheism (that there are many gods of relatively equal worth) and the specifically biblical teaching concerning Jesus as the only begotten Son of God: "[Allah] begetteth not nor is He begotten." For orthodox Islam, no human being, even the greatest of prophets, is anything more than simply a human being and slave/servant of Allah. No one, including Jesus, has the right or authority to address God as Father.

2. How are Jesus and the Holy Spirit connected?

The Bible says:

John 1:32–34 (ESV)

John bore witness: "I saw the Spirit descend from heaven like a dove, and it remained on him. I myself did not know him, but he who sent me to baptize with water said to me, 'He on whom you see the Spirit descend and remain, this is he who baptizes with the Holy Spirit.' And I have seen and have borne witness that this is the Son of God."

Luke 4:17–21 (ESV)

The scroll of the prophet Isaiah was given to him. He unrolled the scroll and found the place where it was written, "The Spirit of the Lord is upon me, because he has anointed me to proclaim good news to the poor. He has sent me to proclaim liberty to the captives and recovering of sight to the blind, to set at liberty those who are oppressed, to proclaim the year of the Lord's favor."

And he rolled up the scroll and gave it back to the attendant and sat down. And the eyes of all in the synagogue were fixed on him. And he began to say to them, "Today this Scripture has been fulfilled in your hearing."

John 15:26 (ESV)

But when the Helper comes, whom I will send to you from the Father, the Spirit of truth, who proceeds from the Father, he will bear witness about me.

The Quran says:

4:171

O people of the Scripture (Jews and Christians)! Do not exceed the limits in your religion, nor say of Allah aught but the truth. The Messiah 'Isa (Jesus), son of Maryam (Mary), was (no more than) a Messenger of Allah and His Word, ("Be!"—and he was) which He bestowed on Maryam (Mary) and a spirit (*Ruh*) from Him; so believe in Allah and His Messengers. Say not: "Three (trinity)!" Cease! (it is) better for you. For Allah is (the only) One *Ilah* (God), Glory be to Him (Far Exalted is He) above having a son. To Him belongs all that is in the heavens and all that is in the earth. And Allah is All-Sufficient as a Disposer of affairs.

2:253

Those Messengers! We preferred some to others; to some of them Allah spoke (directly); others He raised to degrees (of honour); and to 'Isa (Jesus), the son of Maryam (Mary), We gave clear proofs and evidences, and supported him with *Ruh-ul-Qudus* [the Spirit of the Holy One]. If Allah had willed, succeeding generations would not have fought against each other, after clear Verses of Allah had come to them, but they differed—some of them believed and others disbelieved. If Allah had willed, they would not have fought against one another, but Allah does what He likes.

Perspective:

Jesus and the Holy Spirit share an intimate bond, according to the Gospels. In His Upper Room Discourse (John 14—16), Jesus speaks of the Spirit not merely as a "force" or as "the arm of the Lord" but rather as a divine personage. The Spirit will lead the disciples when Jesus has ascended to heaven; He is the "Advocate" (Paraclete) who will dwell within Jesus' followers and guide them into all truth. The same Spirit who empowered Jesus for His public ministry by descending upon Him at His baptism in the symbolic form of a dove, is the one whom Jesus promised to impart to His followers to carry on His work. Only the Son of God has the authority from God the Father to send the Holy Spirit as a gift to the Church for the welfare of the world.

Muhammad did not accept this unique relationship between Jesus and the Holy Spirit. In fact, Muhammad seemed to show an evolving understanding of "the Spirit of the Holy [One]." In early Quranic revelations, the Spirit is not only not divine but is rather an exalted but unnamed spiritual being who seems to take his place among the ranks of angels (heavenly messengers). Only in later revelations does it become clear that the Spirit is none other than the archangel Jibril (Gabriel). Jesus, as one of the great ("preferred") prophets of God, is supported particularly by the Spirit of the Holy One. This passage (2:253) shows Muhammad's clear belief that Jesus stands among an exalted class of messengers, though His relationship with this Spirit is not altogether unique. However, in 4:171 Jesus is spoken of as "a spirit from Him," that is, from God. While this does not seem to be a reference to the same being known elsewhere as the Spirit of the Holy One, it does point to Jesus' uniqueness in the spiritual realm. No other prophet or human being, including Muhammad himself, is ever spoken of as a "spirit from Allah."

3. What revelation has the Spirit inspired?

The Bible says:

John 14:16–17, 26 (NLT)

And I will ask the Father, and he will give you another Advocate, who will never leave you. He is the Holy Spirit, who leads into all truth. The world cannot receive him, because it isn't looking for him and doesn't recognize him. But you know him, because he lives with you now and later will be in you. . . . But when the Father sends the Advocate as my representative—that is, the Holy Spirit—he will teach you everything and will remind you of everything I have told you.

John 16:12–14 (NLT)

There is so much more I want to tell you, but you can't bear it now. When the Spirit of truth comes, he will guide you into all truth. He will not speak on his own but will tell you what he has heard. He will tell you about the future. He will bring me glory by telling you whatever he receives from me.

The Quran says:

42:52

And thus We have sent to you (O Muhammad) *Ruhan* (an Inspiration, and a Mercy) of Our Command. You knew not what is the Book, nor what is Faith? But We have made it (this Qur'an) a light wherewith We guide whosoever of Our slaves We will. And verily, you (O Muhammad) are indeed guiding (mankind) to the Straight Path (i.e. Allah's religion of Islamic Monotheism).

16:102

Say (O Muhammad) *Ruh-ul-Qudus* [Jibrael (Gabriel)] has brought it (the Qur'an) down from your Lord with truth, that it may make firm and strengthen (the Faith of) those who believe and as a guidance and glad tidings to those who have submitted (to Allah as Muslims).

2:97–98

Say (O Muhammad Peace be upon him): "Whoever is an enemy to Jibrael (Gabriel) (let him die in his fury), for indeed he has brought it (this Qur'an) down to your heart by Allah's Permission, confirming what came before it [i.e. the Taurat (Torah) and the Injeel (Gospel)] and guidance and glad tidings for the believers. Whoever is an enemy to Allah, His Angels, His Messengers, Jibrael (Gabriel) and Mikael (Michael), then verily, Allah is an enemy to the disbelievers."

Perspective:

The Quran mentions the Spirit nineteen times. Only late in Muhammad's career is the Spirit equated with the angel Gabriel, as we see in 2:97–98. The primary role of the Spirit in history is to reveal God's message to the prophets, who in turn bring it to their people. Since Gabriel figured so prominently in New Testament encounters bringing revelation to Zachariah and Mary, Muhammad apparently concluded that the Spirit sent from God to bring revelation to the prophets (and so to him as well) must be Gabriel. Since in Islamic thinking God has no partners or equals, this Spirit is never considered divine in the sense of coming from God's essence, but rather is a created being who, like all other created beings, is a slave of God to do His bidding.

In the New Testament, on the other hand, the Spirit is fully divine, sharing those traits equally with the Father and the Son. He is not a creature sent from the throne of God, but God the third member of the Trinity. Hence, He is regularly identified as the "Holy" Spirit. With regard to the work of revelation, His mission is to continue the work of Jesus in the midst of God's people by remaining among and within Jesus' followers, reminding them of Christ's teachings, and leading them into the fullness of truth. Jesus speaks of the Spirit as His representative, and as "another advocate" (John 14:16). The original Greek word for "another" here indicates a second object of the same nature as the first, making clear Jesus' view that the Holy Spirit bears both His nature and His purpose toward the disciples.

Since the death of Muhammad, the Quranic Spirit has no further role (there are to be no further prophets in Islam), but the Holy Spirit of the Bible is fully engaged within and among Jesus' disciples until the new heavens and new earth come in the fullness of glory.

4. What should be the central prayer of believers?

The Bible says:

Matthew 6:9–13 (NIV)
This, then, is how you should pray: "Our Father in heaven, hallowed be your name, your kingdom come, your will be done, on earth as it is in heaven. Give us today our daily bread. And forgive us our debts, as we also have forgiven our debtors. And lead us not into temptation, but deliver us from the evil one."

Luke 11:2–4 (NIV)
He said to them, "When you pray, say: "'Father, hallowed be your name, your kingdom come. Give us each day our daily bread. Forgive us our sins, for we also forgive everyone who sins against us. And lead us not into temptation.'"

The Quran says:

1:1–7
In the Name of Allah, the Most Beneficent, the Most Merciful. All the praises and thanks be to Allah, the Lord of the 'Alamin (mankind, jinns and all that exists). The Most Beneficent, the Most Merciful. The Only Owner (and the Only Ruling Judge) of the Day of Recompense (i.e. the Day of Resurrection) You (Alone) we worship, and You (Alone) we ask for help (for each and everything). Guide us to the Straight Way The Way of those on whom You have bestowed Your Grace, not (the way) of those who earned Your Anger (such as the Jews), nor of those who went astray (such as the Christians).

Perspective:

Jesus teaches on prayer in the Sermon on the Mount, where in Matthew 6 he admonishes disciples that their praying should be done in private so as to starve the impulse to use our relationship with God as a way to impress others. Further, prayer should not be the mere recitation of many words, as if God Himself would be impressed by the mere volume of what we say. Instead, Jesus gives His followers a pattern for prayer found in verses 9–13. It is meant to be prayed by the community together, though certainly it can also be prayed in private. God is addressed as "Our Father in heaven," which of course underscores that all disciples of Jesus form one family under God's Fatherhood. Those who pray this prayer hallow or set apart God's name (or essence) as something to be treasured above all else. They yearn for the full establishment of God's Kingdom in this fallen world, where His will is always joyfully carried out, which happens naturally in heaven. In the second half of the prayer, attention turns to personal intercession. We seek God's provision for our daily material needs, His grace to forgive our moral transgressions, and His guiding power to aid our ongoing battles against temptation. According to Jesus, those who claim to follow Him must become people marked by a forgiving nature. It is impossible to truly receive God's magnanimous, forgiving grace and remain hardhearted toward those who seek forgiveness for whatever ways they may have wronged us. Any refusal to show such grace to others indicates that our hearts have not yet been penetrated by God's mercy.

For Muslims the Quran is understood to be wholly God's direct revelations to Muhammad, which Muhammad in turn recited to his listeners. Yet the opening chapter of the Quran, Surat al-Fatiha, was written as a prayer in which believers address God rather than God addressing human beings. In Islamic practice, this has become the central prayer of Islamic life. It is recited seventeen times daily within the five prescribed prayer times marking every day. Beginning with the *bismillah* ("In the name of God, the merciful, the compassionate"), it addresses God as the Lord who is over all, the One who (again) is merciful and compassionate, the Master of the day of judgment, i.e., the only One who determines the ultimate destinies of all human beings. As with the prayer Jesus taught, this prayer may be separated into two sections: the first offers praise to Allah, this gracious Lord who is also the final Judge. In the fifth verse, the transition occurs from acknowledgment that Allah alone is the One worshipped to a petition for help, especially that Muslims would be guided by God on the straight path—the way of Islam.

Another similarity is that this prayer is meant to be prayed by the community as a whole, rather than just by individuals. The final verse emphasizes the importance of being on the "straight path," the path blessed by God's grace, and contrasts this with the path chosen by those who have earned God's anger by rebelling, and the path chosen by those who have allowed themselves to be misled. Though the text itself does not indicate who comprise these groups, in common Muslim understanding, it is the Jews above all who have earned God's anger, and the Christians who have strayed from God. With this central prayer being recited by Muslims seventeen times daily, it is not surprising that their view of Jews and Christians is generally less than positive.

5. Who among the dead qualify to live forever?

The Bible says:

John 11:25–26 (NKJV)

Jesus said to her, "I am the resurrection and the life. He who believes in Me, though he may die, he shall live. And whoever lives and believes in Me shall never die. Do you believe this?"

The Quran says:

2:154

And say not of those who are killed in the Way of Allah, "They are dead." Nay, they are living, but you perceive (it) not.

3:169

Think not of those who are killed in the Way of Allah as dead. Nay, they are alive, with their Lord, and they have provision.

Perspective:

This New Testament passage occurs in the context of two sisters' grief over the death of their brother Lazarus. Jesus comes to comfort them, but even more to raise Lazarus back to life. In conversation with sister Martha, where she acknowledges her belief that God will raise her brother in the "the resurrection at the last day"—at the end of time (John 11:24), Jesus makes a rather spectacular declaration, "I am the resurrection and the life" (John 11:25). In this, He claims to be the source of eternal life, and promises that any who trust Him with their lives will never succumb to the ultimate destruction of death. In raising Lazarus Jesus demonstrates His power to reverse the reach of physical death. In His own resurrection, He breaks the power of death completely and promises that those who belong to Him will not be condemned by their sins but inherit His eternal life. Conversely, he declares that those who refuse to follow Him are condemned already, and apart from Him have no hope (see John 3:18–21).

According to the Quran, those "killed in the way of Allah" are enjoying the eternity of Paradise even now, though the earthly sight cannot perceive that reality. As is clear from the phrase itself, this promise applies only to a subset of those who die, namely those who are "killed" in the way of Allah. Thus, it is the *mujahid* (the practitioner of *jihad*, one who engages in physical battle to advance the cause of Islam) who receives the assurance of life after death. All other Muslims live with the fragile hope that God will be merciful to them, framed by the fear that He will rather punish them eternally for their sins. According to 19.71–72, all Muslims (not just unbelievers) will be sent to hell by the decree of God. Then He will rescue those who during their lifetimes "used to fear God and were dutiful to Him." The rest of humanity He will leave in hell.

6. How should we address God?

The Bible says:

Matthew 6:9 (ESV)
Pray then like this: "Our Father in heaven, hallowed be your name."

Matthew 7:11 (ESV)
If you then, who are evil, know how to give good gifts to your children, how much more will your Father who is in heaven give good things to those who ask him!

The Quran says:

7:180
And (all) the Most Beautiful Names belong to Allah, so call on Him by them, and leave the company of those who belie or deny (or utter impious speech against) His Names. They will be requited for what they used to do.

59:23–24
He is Allah than Whom there is *La ilaha illa Huwa* (none has the right to be worshipped but He) the King, the Holy, the One Free from all defects, the Giver of security, the Watcher over His creatures, the All-Mighty, the Compeller, the Supreme. Glory be to Allah! (High is He) above all that they associate as partners with Him. He is Allah, the Creator, the Inventor of all things, the Bestower of forms. To Him belong the Best Names. All that is in the heavens and the earth glorify Him. And He is the All-Mighty, the All-Wise.

Perspective:

Of all Jesus' insights about God, perhaps the most unique truth He taught was that human beings could think of God in the personal, intimately relational terms of a heavenly Father. Nowhere in Israel's revelatory history had this ever been taught before. Although God was spoken of sparingly as the Father of Israel as a nation, He was never thought of as the personal God of each Israelite. Jesus taught the disciples to address God as *Abba*, the Aramaic term best rendered in English as "Papa," or in Arabic as "Baba." It is the common family term used both by little children of their fathers and of grown adults toward their beloved family elders. The disciples are welcomed to call God *Abba* because through Jesus, the only begotten Son of the Father, they are adopted into relationship with God as sons and daughters.

For Muslims this is a scandalous, even blasphemous, idea. Numerous times the Quran rejects the notion that God could beget a son, and warns that any who teach such a thing will have the mountains fall upon them with crushing weight and spend their eternities roasting in hell. So stark is the monotheism of the Quran, and so steadfast is Muhammad in his opposition to the polytheism surrounding him in Mecca, that any hint of divine offspring smacks of paganism. It seems clear from other Quranic passages that Muhammad believed Christians to be asserting that God through a sexual relationship with Mary produced Jesus as a literal son of God, which of course the Arabian prophet rejected out of hand. God would never "beget" a son, nor take one (by adoption). Though Jesus holds a place of high esteem in the Quran, He is never more than a mere human slave serving God obediently as a major prophet. According to Islam, Jesus would never call God His Father, for such a claim would elevate Him to a status alongside God, something the Quran expressly forbids to anyone or anything in the creation.

7. How does God view children?

The Bible says:

Mark 10:13–16 (NLT)

One day some parents brought their children to Jesus so he could touch and bless them. But the disciples scolded the parents for bothering him.

When Jesus saw what was happening, he was angry with his disciples. He said to them, "Let the children come to me. Don't stop them! For the Kingdom of God belongs to those who are like these children. I tell you the truth, anyone who doesn't receive the Kingdom of God like a child will never enter it." Then he took the children in his arms and placed his hands on their heads and blessed them.

Luke 10:21 (NLT)

At that same time Jesus was filled with the joy of the Holy Spirit, and he said, "O Father, Lord of heaven and earth, thank you for hiding these things from those who think themselves wise and clever, and for revealing them to the childlike. Yes, Father, it pleased you to do it this way."

The Quran says:

18:46

Wealth and children are the adornment of the life of this world. But the good righteous deeds (five compulsory prayers, deeds of Allah's obedience, good and nice talk, remembrance of Allah with glorification, praises and thanks, etc.), that last, are better with your Lord for rewards and better in respect of hope.

64:14–15

O you who believe! Verily, among your wives and your children there are enemies for you (i.e. may stop you from the obedience of Allah), therefore beware of them! But if you pardon (them) and overlook, and forgive (their faults), then verily, Allah is Oft-Forgiving, Most Merciful. Your wealth and your children are only a trial, whereas Allah! With Him is a great reward (Paradise).

Perspective:

𝔍esus welcomed children into His presence and blessed them. When His disciples sought to protect their Master's time and importance, and rebuked parents for bringing their children for a touch from him, Jesus became indignant, and ordered his disciples to get out of the way so the children could come to him freely. "Do not hinder them," he said in Matthew 19:14, "for the kingdom of heaven belongs to such as these." He went on to underscore that only those who respond to the Kingdom like a child will enter it, and he demonstrated the love of His Father for children by embracing the children who came to Him, and blessing them with the touch of gracious love. In Luke 10, Jesus gives us one glimpse of why God loves children—they claim no standing for themselves apart from God, but live by trust. Because they do not trust in their own wisdom and understanding, but are open to Him, God chooses to reveal Himself to them and to hide His truth from those who revel in their own capacities.

The Quran speaks little about children directly. Muhammad does indeed indicate that wealth and children are good blessings of life, but they are subordinate to the achievement of righteous deeds because such deeds bring the hope of lasting reward from God (18:46). Children, on the other hand, lumped together with properties, can be a distraction from giving one's attentions fully to the service of Allah (63:9). Muhammad's primary concern with regard to wives and children is that they can become enemies of the believer by diverting his attention from his obligations toward the prophet and Allah. In that case, they are a trial for the believer, luring him away from devotion to Allah with whom alone is great reward (64:14–15).

8. Are human beings good or evil by nature?

The Bible says:

Matthew 7:11 (ESV)
If you then, who are evil, know how to give good gifts to your children, how much more will your Father who is in heaven give good things to those who ask him!

Matthew 9:35–36 (ESV)
Jesus went throughout all the cities and villages, teaching in their synagogues and proclaiming the gospel of the kingdom and healing every disease and every affliction. When he saw the crowds, he had compassion for them, because they were harassed and helpless, like sheep without a shepherd.

Matthew 16:17–20 (ESV)
Jesus answered him, "Blessed are you, Simon Bar-Jonah! For flesh and blood has not revealed this to you, but my Father who is in heaven. And I tell you, you are Peter, and on this rock I will build my church, and the gates of hell shall not prevail against it. I will give you the keys of the kingdom of heaven, and whatever you bind on earth shall be bound in heaven, and whatever you loose on earth shall be loosed in heaven." Then he strictly charged the disciples to tell no one that he was the Christ.

The Quran says:

91:7–10
And by Nafs (Adam or a person or a soul, etc.), and Him Who perfected him in proportion; Then He showed him what is wrong for him and what is right for him; Indeed he succeeds who purifies his ownself (i.e. obeys and performs all that Allah ordered, by following the true Faith of Islamic Monotheism and by doing righteous good deeds). And indeed he fails who corrupts his ownself (i.e. disobeys what Allah has ordered by rejecting the true Faith of Islamic Monotheism or by following polytheism, etc. or by doing every kind of evil wicked deeds).

95:4–6
Verily, We created man of the best stature (mould), Then We reduced him to the lowest of the low, Save those who believe (in Islamic Monotheism) and do righteous deeds, then they shall have a reward without end (Paradise).

33:72
Truly, We did offer Al-Amanah (the trust or moral responsibility or honesty and all the duties which Allah has ordained) to the heavens and the earth, and the mountains, but they declined to bear it and were afraid of it (i.e. afraid of Allah's Torment). But man bore it. Verily, he was unjust (to himself) and ignorant (of its results).

32:13
And if We had willed, surely! We would have given every person his guidance, but the Word from Me took effect (about evil-doers), that I will fill Hell with jinn and mankind together.

Perspective:

The teaching of Jesus builds upon the Genesis creation narrative, recognizing that human beings were first created in the image of God and without sin. After choosing to rebel from God, human nature was subsequently warped, so that though the image of God is still recognizable, it is nonetheless marred by a fallen nature. Hence, Jesus shows that it is not external realities that cause evil to invade innocent human hearts but rather the sinful tendency already in the human heart that serves as the fountain producing all manner of loathsome thoughts and actions (Matthew 15:17–20). This does not mean that human beings are incapable of doing good, but that our natures are always tending away from God and because of that, oriented to evil. In contrast, God, who is always and only good, can never entertain or commit evil. This contrast is what Jesus highlights in His encouragement concerning prayer in Matthew 7:11: "If you, then, though you are evil, know how to give good gifts to your children, how much more will your Father in heaven give good gifts to those who ask him!"

In the Quran, Muhammad seems to teach that all human beings are born with equal capacity to follow after God obediently. Human nature is not "fallen" because of the first sin of Adam and Eve. Sin is basically the forgetting of one's responsibility to submit to God. By remembering and obeying the teachings of Muhammad, one eradicates his/her sin, and hopes that God's mercy will prevail. Nevertheless, the Quran also contains strands of fatalistic teaching which uphold the belief that God has already decided each person's destiny, so that nothing in human nature or actions will in the end meaningfully contribute to one's ultimate fate.

9. Can one know God's forgiveness here and now?

The Bible says:

Luke 7:47–50 (NKJV)

"Therefore I say to you, her sins, which are many, are forgiven, for she loved much. But to whom little is forgiven, the same loves little." Then He said to her, "Your sins are forgiven."

And those who sat at the table with Him began to say to themselves, "Who is this who even forgives sins?"

Then He said to the woman, "Your faith has saved you. Go in peace."

Matthew 9:2–7 (NKJV)

Then behold, they brought to Him a paralytic lying on a bed. When Jesus saw their faith, He said to the paralytic, "Son, be of good cheer; your sins are forgiven you."

And at once some of the scribes said within themselves, "This Man blasphemes!"

But Jesus, knowing their thoughts, said, "Why do you think evil in your hearts? For which is easier, to say, 'Your sins are forgiven you,' or to say, 'Arise and walk'? But that you may know that the Son of Man has power on earth to forgive sins"—then He said to the paralytic, "Arise, take up your bed, and go to your house." And he arose and departed to his house.

Luke 19:9–10 (NKJV)

Jesus said to him, "Today salvation has come to this house, because he also is a son of Abraham; for the Son of Man has come to seek and to save that which was lost."

The Quran says:

3:134–136

Those who spend [in Allah's Cause—deeds of charity, alms, etc.] in prosperity and in adversity, who repress anger, and who pardon men; verily, Allah loves *Al-Muhsinun* (the good-doers). And those who, when they have committed *Fahishah* (illegal sexual intercourse etc.) or wronged themselves with evil, remember Allah and ask forgiveness for their sins;—and none can forgive sins but Allah—And do not persist in what (wrong) they have done, while they know. For such, the reward is Forgiveness from their Lord, and Gardens with rivers flowing underneath (Paradise), wherein they shall abide forever. How excellent is this reward for the doers (who do righteous deeds according to Allah's Orders).

4:17

Allah accepts only the repentance of those who do evil in ignorance and foolishness and repent soon afterwards; it is they to whom Allah will forgive and Allah is Ever All-Knower, All-Wise.

5:39

But whosoever repents after his crime and does righteous good deeds (by obeying Allah), then verily, Allah will pardon him (accept his repentance). Verily, Allah is Oft-Forgiving, Most Merciful.

Perspective:

One of Jesus' dramatic claims is the authority to forgive sins in the name of His Father. In Luke 7:37–48, He assures a woman "who had lived a sinful life," based on her penitence and devotion expressed toward Him, that her sins are forgiven (note the present tense). In Matthew 9 (see also Mark 2), Jesus does the same for a paralyzed man. The Jewish onlookers who hear His declarations are astonished, some even offended, understanding that only God can forgive sins. Under their breath, some leaders mutter that Jesus is blaspheming, arrogating to Himself what is only God's by right. But Jesus understands that He was sent by His Father to "seek and save the lost" (Luke 19:10), so in His unique ministry as Messiah and Savior He can pronounce forgiveness on all who come to Him. Reconciliation with God is no longer a future hope but a present reality for those who enter into relationship with Jesus.

The Quran also declares (3:135) that none can forgive sins but Allah. Such forgiveness is seen as a reward (3:136) granted to those who quickly repent after having done wrong in ignorance (4:17), who subsequently demonstrate righteousness through good deeds (5:39). Yet since God's judgments are inscrutable, and since we continue to fall into sin, no one can know whether his/her sins have been forgiven until the final day of judgment. Even Muhammad, according to Islamic tradition, asked his companions to pray for him, that God might forgive his sins on the last day, because "to Allah alone belongs dominion over heaven and earth. He punishes whom He wills and forgives whom He wills" (5:40). No one can presume to know God's mind and heart with regard to an individual's destiny—no one can assure a sinner here and now that God has already forgiven him/her.

10. What is God's vision for marriage?

The Bible says:

Luke 20:35 (NIV)
Those who are considered worthy of taking part in the age to come and in the resurrection from the dead will neither marry nor be given in marriage.

Matthew 19:4–7 (NIV)
"Haven't you read," he replied, "that at the beginning the Creator 'made them male and female,' and said, 'For this reason a man will leave his father and mother and be united to his wife, and the two will become one flesh.' So they are no longer two, but one flesh. Therefore what God has joined together, let no one separate."

"Why then," they asked, "did Moses command that a man give his wife a certificate of divorce and send her away?"

The Quran says:

4:19–20, 24–25
O you who believe! You are forbidden to inherit women against their will, and you should not treat them with harshness, that you may take away part of the *Mahr* (*dowry*) you have given them, unless they commit open illegal sexual intercourse. And live with them honourably. If you dislike them, it may be that you dislike a thing and Allah brings through it a great deal of good. But if you intend to replace a wife by another and you have given one of them a *Qintar* (of gold i.e. a great amount) as *Mahr*, take not the least bit of it back. . . .

Also (forbidden are) women already married, except those (captives and slaves) whom your right hands possess. Thus has Allah ordained for you. All others are lawful, provided you seek (them in marriage) with *Mahr* (bridal money given by the husband to his wife at the time of marriage) from your property, desiring chastity, not committing illegal sexual intercourse, so with those of whom you have enjoyed sexual relations, give them their *Mahr* as prescribed; but if after a *Mahr* is prescribed, you agree mutually (to give more), there is no sin on you. Surely, Allah is Ever All-Knowing, All-Wise. And whoever of you have not the means wherewith to wed free, believing women, they may wed believing girls from among those (captives and slaves) whom your right hands possess, and Allah has full knowledge about your Faith, you are one from another. Wed them with the permission of their own folk (guardians, *Auliya'* or masters) and give them their *Mahr* according to what is reasonable; they should be chaste, not adulterous, nor taking boy-friends. And after they have been taken in wedlock, if they commit illegal sexual intercourse, their punishment is half that for free (unmarried) women.

30:21
And among His Signs is this, that He created for you wives from among yourselves, that you may find repose in them, and He has put between you affection and mercy. Verily, in that are indeed signs for a people who reflect.

2:223
Your wives are a tilth for you, so go to your tilth (have sexual relations with your wives), when or how you will, and send (good deeds, or ask Allah to bestow upon you pious offspring) before you for your ownselves. And fear Allah, and know that you are to meet Him (in the Hereafter), and give good tidings to the believers (O Muhammad).

Perspective:

In Matthew 19, when Jesus is tested by some teachers of the Law regarding the permissibility of divorce, he responds by changing the focus of discussion to the purpose of marriage. Quoting from the creation narrative in Genesis 1—2, Jesus highlights that God created humans as male and female with the express purpose that in adulthood couples would form by leaving their families of origin to create a new relationship and life together. Their joining in marriage is symbolized and consummated by their sexual union, which in some mystical, suprarational way makes them one "organism" in God's eyes. Hence, they can no longer be simply separated after such a union by a decree of divorce. The one-flesh covenant of marriage is meant to be lifelong, reflecting God's own triune nature as a "being-in-relationship" as well as His faithful covenant with His people. Divorce therefore is seen as a betrayal of God's original will and intent, not simply as a contractual decision between individuals that frees them up from their prior vows. Marriage is meant for the welfare and enjoyment of a man and woman together. Muhammad offers detailed instructions to men about marriage, including the provision of a dowry, the impermissibility of marrying a nonbeliever, and the permissibility of marrying one's own slave girls. The initiative in marrying belongs wholly to the man, and wives are viewed primarily as a benefit Allah has provided for the man's pleasure. In 2:223, wives are pictured as fields to be plowed by their husbands—imagery that is clearly understood to refer to sexual intercourse which a husband is permitted to engage in with his wife or wives whenever he desires. The marriage relationship, while important, is never envisioned as a lifelong covenant whose rupture is an act of sin, but rather as a contract which can be ended by the husband whenever he wishes.

11. Will there be marriages in heaven?

The Bible says:

Luke 20:34–36 (ESV)

Jesus said to them, "The sons of this age marry and are given in marriage, but those who are considered worthy to attain to that age and to the resurrection from the dead neither marry nor are given in marriage, for they cannot die anymore, because they are equal to angels and are sons of God, being sons of the resurrection."

The Quran says:

36:55–56

Verily, the dwellers of the Paradise, that Day, will be busy in joyful things. They and their wives will be in pleasant shade, reclining on thrones.

40:8

Our Lord! And make them enter the *'Adn* (Eden) Paradise (everlasting Gardens) which you have promised them, and to the righteous among their fathers, their wives, and their offspring! Verily, You are the All-Mighty, the All-Wise.

43:70

Enter Paradise, you and your wives, in happiness.

Perspective:

In Luke 20, some Sadducees (who did not believe in the resurrection of the dead) seek to stymie Jesus with a hypothetical question about a woman who had been successively married to seven brothers, each of whom had died and left her as a widow then married by the next in line. In heaven, they wondered, whose wife would she be since all seven had been married to her? Jesus unequivocally teaches in response that marriage is a covenant relationship that continues in this age but does not extend to heaven. Indeed, He declares not only that earthly marriages no longer continue in heaven but that there will be no new marriages among the redeemed in heaven. The covenant of marriage will apparently be superseded by a new quality of relationship among God's people which will be appropriate to their perfect and eternal natures.

According to the Quran, in contrast, those who dwell in Paradise "together with their wives" will be "in pleasant shade, reclining on thrones." In addition to their earthly wives, men in heaven will be rewarded by marriages to *houri* (44:54; 52:20—these are beautiful, young, doe-eyed, submissive, virgin women whom Allah has created in heaven specifically to fulfill the believers' sexual appetites). They are amply endowed (78:33) and remain perpetual virgins, no matter how many times their husbands have sex with them.

12. How does God feel about divorce?

The Bible says:

Matthew 5:31-32 (NIV)
It has been said, "Anyone who divorces his wife must give her a certificate of divorce." But I tell you that anyone who divorces his wife, except for sexual immorality, makes her the victim of adultery, and anyone who marries a divorced woman commits adultery.

Matthew 19:7-9 (NIV)
"Why then," they asked, "did Moses command that a man give his wife a certificate of divorce and send her away?"

Jesus replied, "Moses permitted you to divorce your wives because your hearts were hard. But it was not this way from the beginning. I tell you that anyone who divorces his wife, except for sexual immorality, and marries another woman commits adultery."

The Quran says:

4:20
But if you intend to replace a wife by another and you have given one of them a *Cantar* (of gold i.e. a great amount) as *Mahr*, take not the least bit of it back; would you take it wrongfully without a right and (with) a manifest sin?

2:226-228
Those who take an oath not to have sexual relation with their wives must wait four months, then if they return (change their idea in this period), verily, Allah is Oft-Forgiving, Most Merciful. And if they decide upon divorce, then Allah is All-Hearer, All-Knower. And divorced women shall wait (as regards their marriage) for three menstrual periods, and it is not lawful for them to conceal what Allah has created in their wombs, if they believe in Allah and the Last Day. And their husbands have the better right to take them back in that period, if they wish for reconciliation. And they (women) have rights (over their husbands as regards living expenses, etc.) similar (to those of their husbands) over them (as regards obedience and respect, etc.) to what is reasonable, but men have a degree (of responsibility) over them. And Allah is All-Mighty, All-Wise.

2:229-230
The divorce is twice, after that, either you retain her on reasonable terms or release her with kindness. And it is not lawful for you (men) to take back (from your wives) any of your *Mahr* (bridal money given by the husband to his wife at the time of marriage) which you have given them, except when both parties fear that they would be unable to keep the limits ordained by Allah (e.g. to deal with each other on a fair basis). Then if you fear that they would not be able to keep the limits ordained by Allah, then there is no sin on either of them if she gives back (the *Mahr* or a part of it) for her *Al-Khul'* (divorce). These are the limits ordained by Allah, so do

not transgress them. And whoever transgresses the limits ordained by Allah, then such are the *Zalimun* (wrong-doers, etc.). And if he has divorced her (the third time), then she is not lawful unto him thereafter until she has married another husband. Then, if the other husband divorces her, it is no sin on both of them that they reunite, provided they feel that they can keep the limits ordained by Allah. These are the limits of Allah, which He makes plain for the people who have knowledge.

Perspective:

According to the Quran, marriage is a contract entered into by a man and a woman. The two are not equal parties. The wife has "honorable rights," but the husband has "a degree above" her. Indeed, the Quran gives him permission to have up to four wives concurrently; wives may only have one husband. Generally, it is the husband who can initiate divorce, and he can finalize it by declaring three times, "I divorce you." If his wife is still of childbearing years, she must be isolated for three months (three periods) to ensure that she is not pregnant with his child before the divorce is finalized. What was hers before the marriage is restored to her (less what she has used up during the marriage). Once the divorce has taken place, the man may not remarry his former wife unless in the interim time she has been married to and divorced by another man.

Jesus' teaching is very different. Following the teaching of the Torah, He describes marriage not as a contract which can be broken by one or both parties but as a covenant sealed before God. In the Matthew 5 passage, He refers back to a practice tolerated in Moses' day—that men could divorce their wives by writing them a bill of divorce if they found "something indecent" in them (see Deuteronomy 24:1–4)—but He condemns this practice as being out of step with God's purposes.

Elsewhere (Matthew 19:3–9), Jesus makes clear that Moses approved divorce only as a concession because of his people's hardness of heart, but "it was not this way from the beginning" (19:8). Instead, marriage is to be treated as an unbreakable union, which God has blessed and made inviolable: "What God has joined together, let no one separate" (19:6). Jesus makes it clear that those who engage in divorce (except in the case of sexual infidelity) and who then remarry, become adulterers, because in God's eyes their original marriage covenant has not been undone, so in sleeping with a new partner they are engaging in sexual relations with someone other than their true spouse.

13. May a man marry more than one woman?

The Bible says:

Mark 10:11–12 (NKJV)

So He said to them, "Whoever divorces his wife and marries another commits adultery against her. And if a woman divorces her husband and marries another, she commits adultery."

Matthew 19:4–6 (NKJV)

He answered and said to them, "Have you not read that He who made them at the beginning 'made them male and female,' and said, 'For this reason a man shall leave his father and mother and be joined to his wife, and the two shall become one flesh'? So then, they are no longer two but one flesh. Therefore what God has joined together, let not man separate."

The Quran says:

4:3, 129

And if you fear that you shall not be able to deal justly with the orphan-girls, then marry (other) women of your choice, two or three, or four but if you fear that you shall not be able to deal justly (with them), then only one or (the captives and the slaves) that your right hands possess. That is nearer to prevent you from doing injustice...

You will never be able to do perfect justice between wives even if it is your ardent desire, so do not incline too much to one of them (by giving her more of your time and provision) so as to leave the other hanging (i.e. neither divorced nor married). And if you do justice, and do all that is right and fear Allah by keeping away from all that is wrong, then Allah is Ever Oft-Forgiving, Most Merciful.

Perspective:

esus appeals to God's original intention in the creation of Adam and Eve as the model for marriage relationships. Marriage is meant to be a partnership of equals, who complement each other as male and female. In this union, two become one, and are not to be separated. Hence, not only is divorce against God's will, but polygamy is proscribed as an unsustainable intrusion into the one-flesh relationship of the original marriage between one man and one woman. As such, the same argument from Jesus concerning divorce (Mark 10:11–12) would apply to polygamy: "Anyone who divorces his wife and marries another woman commits adultery against her."

Muhammad in the text of the Quran assumes that men will normally have up to four wives, though 4:3 counsels that if a husband does not feel he can treat them all fairly then he may marry only one (in addition to any slave girls he may have, with whom he is free to engage in sexual relations as he chooses). Interestingly, later in this same chapter Muhammad admits that no man will ever relate to multiple wives with equal justice, but if he attempts to do his best, that will suffice. Wives, of course, do not have the option of several contemporaneous husbands.

14. How are we to treat our enemies?

The Bible says:

Matthew 5:43–45 (ESV)
You have heard that it was said, "You shall love your neighbor and hate your enemy." But I say to you, Love your enemies and pray for those who persecute you, so that you may be sons of your Father who is in heaven. For he makes his sun rise on the evil and on the good, and sends rain on the just and on the unjust.

Luke 6:35–36 (ESV)
Love your enemies, and do good, and lend, expecting nothing in return, and your reward will be great, and you will be sons of the Most High, for he is kind to the ungrateful and the evil. Be merciful, even as your Father is merciful.

The Quran says:

5:33
The recompense of those who wage war against Allah and His Messenger and do mischief in the land is only that they shall be killed or crucified or their hands and their feet be cut off on the opposite sides, or be exiled from the land. That is their disgrace in this world, and a great torment is theirs in the Hereafter.

4:84
Then fight (O Muhammad) in the Cause of Allah, you are not tasked (held responsible) except for yourself, and incite the believers (to fight along with you), it may be that Allah will restrain the evil might of the disbelievers. And Allah is Stronger in Might and Stronger in punishing.

2:191
And kill them wherever you find them, and turn them out from where they have turned you out. And *Al-Fitnah* is worse than killing. And fight not with them at *Al-Masjid-al-Haram* (the sanctuary at Makkah), unless they (first) fight you there. But if they attack you, then kill them. Such is the recompense of the disbelievers.

Perspective:

Contrary to the prevailing views of his day, Jesus expands the definition of "neighbor" to include one's enemies (see Matthew 5:43–48). To obey the divine command to love one's neighbor means to show love and care even to those who seek our downfall or destruction. As justification for this teaching Jesus points to the actions of God as our Father. He provides sun and rain in equal measure to the righteous and unrighteous; He demonstrates kindness in manifold ways to the ungrateful and wicked (see Matthew 5:45). If we are truly His children, led by His Spirit, we will demonstrate this same character of mercy toward those who are not similarly inclined in their attitudes and actions toward us. Such love cannot be manufactured by the fallen human heart, and therefore glorifies God by pointing to Him as its source.

The Quran frequently depicts as enemies those who refuse to submit to Allah, who stand opposed to the advance of Islam, who themselves reject the claims of Muhammad to be a true prophet. The prevailing teaching of Muhammad is that such enemies are to be shown no mercy unless and until they repent and submit to the authority of Islam; hence the widespread commands for Muslims to fight (in the armed struggle of *jihad*) against all the enemies of the Prophet. Absent is any teaching that Muslims should pray for the welfare of their persecutors, nor engage in doing good to their enemies. Mercy may be shown to a conquered enemy (who is willing to submit to the laws of Islam as a slave) but unending warfare is commanded against those who will not submit until either they are killed in battle or conquered in victory.

15. How should adultery be punished?

The Bible says:

John 8:3–11 (NLT)

As he was speaking, the teachers of religious law and the Pharisees brought a woman who had been caught in the act of adultery. They put her in front of the crowd.

"Teacher," they said to Jesus, "this woman was caught in the act of adultery. The law of Moses says to stone her. What do you say?"

They were trying to trap him into saying something they could use against him, but Jesus stooped down and wrote in the dust with his finger. They kept demanding an answer, so he stood up again and said, "All right, but let the one who has never sinned throw the first stone!" Then he stooped down again and wrote in the dust.

When the accusers heard this, they slipped away one by one, beginning with the oldest, until only Jesus was left in the middle of the crowd with the woman. Then Jesus stood up again and said to the woman, "Where are your accusers? Didn't even one of them condemn you?"

"No, Lord," she said.

And Jesus said, "Neither do I. Go and sin no more."

The Quran says:

17:32

And come not near to the unlawful sexual intercourse. Verily, it is a *Fahishah* [i.e. anything that transgresses its limits (a great sin)], and an evil way (that leads one to Hell unless Allah forgives him).

24:2

The woman and the man guilty of illegal sexual intercourse, flog each of them with a hundred stripes. Let not pity withhold you in their case, in a punishment prescribed by Allah, if you believe in Allah and the Last Day. And let a party of the believers witness their punishment. (This punishment is for unmarried persons guilty of the above crime but if married persons commit it, the punishment is to stone them to death, according to Allah's Law).

Perspective:

In John 8, when a group of Jewish leaders brought an adulterous woman to Jesus seeking His ruling on how they should deal with her, they believed they had caught Jesus on the horns of a dilemma. All of them, including Jesus, knew that God's Law commanded death by stoning for those guilty of this sin. Yet their desire was really not the upholding of the Law, for in that case they would have also brought the man who was party to the adultery. Instead, they wanted Jesus either to command her execution (which would raise doubts in the minds of the crowds about His message of God's love and mercy) or to command her release (which would put Him at odds with God's revelation and raise questions about His claims to represent God). By ordering the stoning to be commenced only by those who were guilty of no sin themselves, Jesus reminds us all that only God has the authority to condemn sinners, and that His preference is to redeem rather than to destroy. He offers forgiveness to those who repent and seek a new start of obedience to His will.

This is clearly demonstrated by what happens after the crowd of accusers melts away and the adulteress is left alone with Jesus, the only Sinless One among the human race, the only one with the authority to pronounce the condemnation of the Law. Instead, he offers her the chance to begin again, and to live a new kind of life in relationship to God. Adultery is a serious offense to God, but its punishment has been borne by the Crucified One "who had no sin but became sin for us, so that in him we might become the righteousness of God" (2 Corinthians 5:21).

The Quran parallels the Law of Moses in holding all sexual sin to be a serious offense before God. The unmarried who engage in sex together are to be flogged with a hundred lashes. The married who have sex with anyone other than their spouses commit adultery, and this is a capital offense to be punished by stoning. Muhammad holds out the possibility that an adulterer might be forgiven at the last judgment, but commands that the dictates of the laws of Islam must be carried out in this present world. Adultery is to be punished with the sentence of death.

16. Should we fast nowadays? If so, how?

The Bible says:

Matthew 6:16–18 (NKJV)
When you fast, do not be like the hypocrites, with a sad countenance. For they disfigure their faces that they may appear to men to be fasting. Assuredly, I say to you, they have their reward. But you, when you fast, anoint your head and wash your face, so that you do not appear to men to be fasting, but to your Father who is in the secret place; and your Father who sees in secret will reward you openly.

Mark 2:18–20 (NKJV)
The disciples of John and of the Pharisees were fasting. Then they came and said to Him, "Why do the disciples of John and of the Pharisees fast, but Your disciples do not fast?"

And Jesus said to them, "Can the friends of the bridegroom fast while the bridegroom is with them? As long as they have the bridegroom with them they cannot fast. But the days will come when the bridegroom will be taken away from them, and then they will fast in those days."

The Quran says:

2:183–185, 187
O you who believe! Observing *As-Saum* (the fasting) is prescribed for you as it was prescribed for those before you, that you may become *Al-Muttaqun* (the pious). [Observing *Saum* (fasts)] for a fixed number of days, but if any of you is ill or on a journey, the same number (should be made up) from other days. And as for those who can fast with difficulty, (e.g. an old man, etc.), they have (a choice either to fast or) to feed a *Miskin* (poor person) (for every day). But whoever does good of his own accord, it is better for him. And that you fast, it is better for you if only you know. The month of Ramadan in which was revealed the Qur'an, a guidance for mankind and clear proofs for the guidance and the criterion (between right and wrong). So whoever of you sights (the crescent on the first night of) the month (of Ramadan), he must observe *Saum* (fasts) that month, and whoever is ill or on a journey, the same number [of days which one did not observe *Saum* (fasts) must be made up] from other days. Allah intends for you ease, and He does not want to make things difficult for you. (He wants that you) must complete the same number (of days), and that you must magnify Allah for having guided you so that you may be grateful to Him. . . .

It is made lawful for you to have sexual relations with your wives on the night of *As-Saum* (the fasts). They are *Libas* [i.e. body cover, or screen], for you and you are the same for them... So now have sexual relations with them and seek that which Allah has ordained for you (offspring), and eat and drink until the white thread (light) of dawn appears to you distinct from the black thread (darkness of night), then complete your *Saum* (fast) till the nightfall. These are the limits (set) by Allah, so approach them not. (See 2:196 for specific fasting requirements related to the Hajj pilgrimage.)

Perspective:

We do not see instances of the disciples of Jesus fasting during His three years of ministry with them. This is something that caused some observers to wonder about Jesus' legitimacy as a spiritual leader (see Mark 2:18). Jesus' response is that fasting has a proper time and place, but not during times of joy and celebration. His presence with the disciples precludes their fasting; but when He is taken from them (i.e., in death), then fasting will be natural and appropriate. In His general teaching on fasting in the Sermon on the Mount, Jesus makes clear that He expects His followers to fast ("When you fast," not "If you fast"—Matthew 6:16). In line with His teaching on praying and giving, Jesus commands His followers to practice fasting privately and without drawing any attention to themselves. In fact, He counsels them to take special care to keep people from concluding that they are undertaking any ascetic activity, and promises that their heavenly Father, who sees what happens in secret, will appropriately reward them for their private piety (see Matthew 6:16–18).

In the Quran, fasting is taught as an obligation to God which all Muslims are to engage in for the month of Ramadan (the ninth month of the Muslim lunar calendar). Exceptions are made for the elderly, infirm and those who are in the midst of a journey during this time. However, the equivalent days missed are to be made up later in the year, or in the case of the elderly, an amount equivalent to the cost of their daily fare is to be donated to the poor for each day of fasting from which they abstained. Those who fast are to abstain from food, drink and sexual activity from sunrise to sunset for the whole month; they are encouraged to enjoy these necessities and pleasures, however, from sunset to sunrise. Additional fasting is prescribed during and after the Hajj pilgrimage for those too poor to offer the animal sacrifice required of pilgrims. The specified number of days which they fast becomes their sacrificial offering to Allah instead.

17. Should we give alms?

The Bible says:

Matthew 6:1–4 (NIV)

Be careful not to practice your righteousness in front of others to be seen by them. If you do, you will have no reward from your Father in heaven.

So when you give to the needy, do not announce it with trumpets, as the hypocrites do in the synagogues and on the streets, to be honored by others. Truly I tell you, they have received their reward in full. But when you give to the needy, do not let your left hand know what your right hand is doing, so that your giving may be in secret. Then your Father, who sees what is done in secret, will reward you.

Luke 11:37–42 (NIV)

When Jesus had finished speaking, a Pharisee invited him to eat with him; so he went in and reclined at the table. But the Pharisee was surprised when he noticed that Jesus did not first wash before the meal.

Then the Lord said to him, "Now then, you Pharisees clean the outside of the cup and dish, but inside you are full of greed and wickedness. You foolish people! Did not the one who made the outside make the inside also? But now as for what is inside you—be generous to the poor, and everything will be clean for you.

"Woe to you Pharisees, because you give God a tenth of your mint, rue and all other kinds of garden herbs, but you neglect justice and the love of God. You should have practiced the latter without leaving the former undone."

The Quran says:

2:263, 270

Kind words and forgiving of faults are better than *Sadaqah* (charity) followed by injury. And Allah is Rich (Free of all wants) and He is Most-Forbearing....

And whatever you spend for spendings (e.g., in *Sadaqah*—charity, etc. for Allah's Cause) or whatever vow you make, be sure Allah knows it all. And for the *Zalimun* (wrong-doers, etc.) there are no helpers.

9:79

Those who defame such of the believers who give charity (in Allah's Cause) voluntarily, and those who could not find to give charity (in Allah's Cause) except what is available to them, so they mock at them (believers), Allah will throw back their mockery on them, and they shall have a painful torment.

24:56

And perform *As-Salat* (Iqamat-as-Salat), and give *Zakat* and obey the Messenger (Muhammad) that you may receive mercy (from Allah).

57:18
Verily, those who give *Sadaqat* (i.e. *Zakat* and alms, etc.), men and women, and lend to Allah a goodly loan, it shall be increased manifold (to their credit), and theirs shall be an honourable good reward (i.e. Paradise).

58:12
O you who believe! When you (want to) consult the Messenger (Muhammad) in private, spend something in charity before your private consultation. That will be better and purer for you. But if you find not (the means for it), then verily, Allah is Oft-Forgiving, Most Merciful.

Perspective:

As with fasting, almsgiving is an act of piety which Jesus expects all His followers to practice without fanfare. The popular statement, "Do not let your left hand know what your right hand is doing," comes from Jesus' teaching that our giving is to be done so unobtrusively that were it possible, one hand would not know that the other had been used to give alms. While almsgiving is important, it must never become a mechanical act leading to a self-satisfied pretension toward righteousness. In Luke 11, Jesus castigates some Pharisees for their fixation with following the Law minutely by giving away a tenth even of the herbs they grow in their gardens while completely ignoring the weightier matters of the Law (such as justice and the love of God). The latter, Jesus teaches, are more important, though the former are not to be sidestepped either.

In the Quran, Muhammad teaches two kinds of giving: *zakat* is the mandatory giving expected of all obedient Muslims. *Sadaqat* is charity above and beyond what is required. While it is permitted to make public one's charitable gifts, Allah will expunge some of the sins of those who keep their giving secret. It is always wrong to remind the poor of one's generosity, or to seek their harm in any way after showing them charity. In 2:263 is the declaration that kind words and forgiveness are much more valuable than charity followed by ill-will. Muslims are encouraged to see their almsgiving as a loan of their own money to Allah, which He will repay, multiplied many times over, in Paradise.

18. Should we take oaths before God?

The Bible says:

Matthew 5:33–37 (NLT)

You have also heard that our ancestors were told, "You must not break your vows; you must carry out the vows you make to the Lord." But I say, do not make any vows! Do not say, "By heaven!" because heaven is God's throne. And do not say, "By the earth!" because the earth is his footstool. And do not say, "By Jerusalem!" for Jerusalem is the city of the great King. Do not even say, "By my head!" for you can't turn one hair white or black. Just say a simple, "Yes, I will," or "No, I won't." Anything beyond this is from the evil one.

Matthew 23:16–22 (NLT)

Blind guides! What sorrow awaits you! For you say that it means nothing to swear "by God's Temple," but that it is binding to swear "by the gold in the Temple." Blind fools! Which is more important—the gold or the Temple that makes the gold sacred? And you say that to swear "by the altar" is not binding, but to swear "by the gifts on the altar" is binding. How blind! For which is more important—the gift on the altar or the altar that makes the gift sacred? When you swear "by the altar," you are swearing by it and by everything on it. And when you swear "by the Temple," you are swearing by it and by God, who lives in it. And when you swear "by heaven," you are swearing by the throne of God and by God, who sits on the throne.

The Quran says:

51:1

By (the winds) that scatter dust.

74:32–34

Nay, and by the moon, And by the night when it withdraws, And by the dawn when it brightens,

90:1

I swear by this city (Makkah);

91:1

And by the sun and its brightness;

2:224–225

And make not Allah's (Name) an excuse in your oaths against your doing good and acting piously, and making peace among mankind. And Allah is All-Hearer, All-Knower (i.e. do not swear much and if you have sworn against doing something good then give an expiation for the oath and do good). Allah will not call you to account for that which is unintentional in your oaths, but He will call you to account for that which your hearts have earned. And Allah is Oft-Forgiving, Most-Forbearing.

Perspective:

Jesus teaches that His followers should be such people of integrity that they always keep their word ("All you need to say is simply 'Yes' or 'No'"—Matthew 5:37). By this He intensifies the Old Testament command that oaths made to God are to be fulfilled—not only oaths, but all our declarations are to show transparency and integrity, not just vows made to God. In Matthew 23, He decries making vows which are only as binding as the value of that to which they appeal—so that swearing by the Temple is less binding than swearing by the gold which adorns the Temple. In this sense, all oaths (whatever one might swear by) are oaths before God, because God is the source and owner of whatever one may cite as the guarantor of that oath.

The Quran is replete with oaths which Allah swears as a means of underscoring the truthfulness of what He is revealing. This contrasts with biblical understanding (see especially Hebrews 6:13), where God cannot swear by anything less than His own name, for there is nothing greater by which to bind His promises. As Allah Himself makes oaths, it is expected that Muslims as well will engage in taking vows of various kinds. But Muslims are not to make oaths in the name of God that excuse them from acting piously or righteously toward others (much like the practice enjoined by certain Pharisees who taught that men could declare their possessions as "Corban (that is, devoted to God)", and use that as a way to avoid the responsibility of caring materially for their elderly parents [see Mark 7:11–12]). Nor are they to intentionally break any of their oaths. For such behavior Allah will punish them, unless they take appropriate steps to make expiation for broken vows by feeding the poor or fasting, depending on their means.

19. What signs point to the imminent end of the world?

The Bible says:

Luke 21:10–28 (ESV)

Then he said to them, "Nation will rise against nation, and kingdom against kingdom. There will be great earthquakes, and in various places famines and pestilences. And there will be terrors and great signs from heaven. But before all this they will lay their hands on you and persecute you, delivering you up to the synagogues and prisons, and you will be brought before kings and governors for my name's sake. This will be your opportunity to bear witness. Settle it therefore in your minds not to meditate beforehand how to answer, for I will give you a mouth and wisdom, which none of your adversaries will be able to withstand or contradict. You will be delivered up even by parents and brothers and relatives and friends, and some of you they will put to death. You will be hated by all for my name's sake. But not a hair of your head will perish. By your endurance you will gain your lives.

"But when you see Jerusalem surrounded by armies, then know that its desolation has come near. Then let those who are in Judea flee to the mountains, and let those who are inside the city depart, and let not those who are out in the country enter it, for these are days of vengeance, to fulfill all that is written. Alas for women who are pregnant and for those who are nursing infants in those days! For there will be great distress upon the earth and wrath against this people. They will fall by the edge of the sword and be led captive among all nations, and Jerusalem will be trampled underfoot by the Gentiles, until the times of the Gentiles are fulfilled.

"And there will be signs in sun and moon and stars, and on the earth distress of nations in perplexity because of the roaring of the sea and the waves, people fainting with fear and with foreboding of what is coming on the world. For the powers of the heavens will be shaken. And then they will see the Son of Man coming in a cloud with power and great glory. Now when these things begin to take place, straighten up and raise your heads, because your redemption is drawing near."

(See Matthew 24:3-31 for further teaching by Jesus on signs of the world's end.)

The Quran says:

69:13–18

Then when the Trumpet will be blown with one blowing (the first one), And the earth and the mountains shall be removed from their places, and crushed with a single crushing, Then on that Day shall the (Great) Event befall, And the heaven will split asunder, for that Day it (the heaven will be frail (weak), and torn up, And the angels will be on its sides, and eight angels will, that Day, bear the Throne of your Lord above them. That Day shall you be brought to Judgement, not a secret of you will be hidden.

73:17–18
Then how can you avoid the punishment, if you disbelieve, on a Day that will make the children grey-headed (i.e. the Day of Resurrection)? Whereon the heaven will be cleft asunder? His Promise is certainly to be accomplished.

77:8–13
Then when the stars lose their lights; And when the heaven is cleft asunder; And when the mountains are blown away; And when the Messengers are gathered to their time appointed; For what Day are these signs postponed? For the Day of sorting out (the men of Paradise from the men destined for Hell).

82:1–5
When the heaven is cleft asunder. And when the stars have fallen and scattered; And when the seas are burst forth; And when the graves are turned upside down (and they bring out their contents) (Then) a person will know what he has sent forward and (what he has) left behind (of good or bad deeds).

Perspective:

Jesus points to widespread persecution of His followers and the increasing descent of human civilization into evil as precursors to the end. Such cultural upheavals will be accompanied by natural cataclysms. In the midst of all this, the gospel will still go forth to the world. Many false prophets will arise to make self-serving claims; others will claim to have seen the Messiah in secret locations. But when the Messiah comes, His appearance will not be in private or simply to a small group. Instead, as lightning is visible to all from horizon to horizon, so the coming of the Son of Man will be apparent to all. His appearance will signal the end of this age.

Muhammad does not speak much in the Quran of precursors to the Day of Judgment, but offers a great deal of apocalyptic imagery to describe the cataclysmic ending of creation and the arrival of divine judgment to heaven or hell. Mountains will be pulverized, earthquakes will destroy the land, stars will be extinguished, the heavens will be rent asunder and eight angels bearing the throne of God will descend to a decimated creation, at which time God will call all human beings to account.

The Quran knows nothing of the return of any leader sent by God to usher in these last days, although Muslim traditions assert variously that Jesus or the *Mahdi* (correctly "Guided One"), or both will return to rule the world at the head of the Islamic community and so prepare humankind for the Day of Judgment/Day of Resurrection.

20. Must we wash our bodies before we can rightly approach God?

The Bible says:

Matthew 23:25–28 (NIV)

Woe to you, teachers of the law and Pharisees, you hypocrites! You clean the outside of the cup and dish, but inside they are full of greed and self-indulgence. Blind Pharisee! First clean the inside of the cup and dish, and then the outside also will be clean.

Woe to you, teachers of the law and Pharisees, you hypocrites! You are like whitewashed tombs, which look beautiful on the outside but on the inside are full of the bones of the dead and everything unclean. In the same way, on the outside you appear to people as righteous but on the inside you are full of hypocrisy and wickedness.

Luke 11:37–41 (NIV)

When Jesus had finished speaking, a Pharisee invited him to eat with him; so he went in and reclined at the table. But the Pharisee was surprised when he noticed that Jesus did not first wash before the meal.

Then the Lord said to him, "Now then, you Pharisees clean the outside of the cup and dish, but inside you are full of greed and wickedness. You foolish people! Did not the one who made the outside make the inside also? But now as for what is inside you—be generous to the poor, and everything will be clean for you."

The Quran says:

4:43

O you who believe! Approach not *As-Salat* (the prayer) when you are in a drunken state until you know (the meaning) of what you utter, nor when you are in a state of *Janaba*, (i.e. in a state of sexual impurity and have not yet taken a bath) except when travelling on the road (without enough water, or just passing through a mosque), till you wash your whole body. And if you are ill, or on a journey, or one of you comes after answering the call of nature, or you have been in contact with women (by sexual relations) and you find no water, perform *Tayammum* with clean earth and rub therewith your faces and hands (*Tayammum*). Truly, Allah is Ever Oft-Pardoning, Oft-Forgiving.

5:6

O you who believe! When you intend to offer *As-Salat* (the prayer), wash your faces and your hands (forearms) up to the elbows, rub (by passing wet hands over) your heads, and (wash) your feet up to ankles. If you are in a state of *Janaba* (i.e. had a sexual discharge), purify yourself (bathe your whole body). But if you are ill or on a journey or any of you comes from answering the call of nature, or you have been in contact with women (i.e. sexual intercourse) and you find no water, then perform *Tayammum* with clean earth and rub therewith your faces and hands. Allah does not want to place you in difficulty, but He wants to purify you, and to complete His Favour on you that you may be thankful.

Perspective:

"Cleanliness is next to godliness" came to prominence in the English language through the Puritans, but as much as it may be good advice, it does not find its roots in the Bible, or specifically in Jesus' teaching in Luke 11:37–41. Jesus is more concerned about the state of the heart than that of the body when it comes to knowing God. The laws of ceremonial cleansing had become for the Pharisees a means of promoting self-righteousness at the expense of cleansing their hearts of evil. So Jesus speaks of them as whitewashed tombs or cups whose outsides are clean, but inner surfaces are soiled. Instead of appearing righteous but hiding greed, hypocrisy, self-indulgence and wickedness, we should strive for God's intention that we show qualities of goodness from within. It is not physical filth on our bodies that hinders us from approaching God; the moral and spiritual filth in our souls presents a barrier we cannot overcome apart from the cleansing power of Christ's blood shed for our sins.

In the Quran, Allah demands that those who come to Him in prayer must be in a state of ritual cleanliness. There is a multiplicity of things which bring one into impurity, but the most common are sexual activity (even with one's spouse), illness, "answering the call of nature," or having been on a journey. Commands are given as to how one is to wash in order to prepare for prayer, because Allah does not want to place those praying in jeopardy but rather desires to purify them so that they may fulfill their responsibilities.

21. Has God forbidden the eating of certain foods?

The Bible says:

Mark 7:14–19 (ESV)

He called the people to him again and said to them, "Hear me, all of you, and understand: There is nothing outside a person that by going into him can defile him, but the things that come out of a person are what defile him." And when he had entered the house and left the people, his disciples asked him about the parable. And he said to them, "Then are you also without understanding? Do you not see that whatever goes into a person from outside cannot defile him, since it enters not his heart but his stomach, and is expelled?" (Thus he declared all foods clean.)

The Quran says:

5:3

Forbidden to you (for food) are: Al-Maytatah (the dead animals—cattle-beast not slaughtered), blood, the flesh of swine, and the meat of that which has been slaughtered as a sacrifice for others than Allah, or has been slaughtered for idols, etc., or on which Allah's Name has not been mentioned while slaughtering, and that which has been killed by strangling, or by a violent blow, or by a headlong fall, or by the goring of horns—and that which has been (partly) eaten by a wild animal—unless you are able to slaughter it (before its death)—and that which is sacrificed (slaughtered) on An-Nusub (stone altars). (Forbidden) also is to use arrows seeking luck or decision, (all) that is Fisqun (disobedience of Allah and sin). This day, those who disbelieved have given up all hope of your religion, so fear them not, but fear Me. This day, I have perfected your religion for you, completed My Favour upon you, and have chosen for you Islam as your religion. But as for him who is forced by severe hunger, with no inclination to sin (such can eat these above-mentioned meats), then surely, Allah is Oft-Forgiving, Most Merciful.

6:121

Eat not (O believers) of that (meat) on which Allah's Name has not been pronounced (at the time of the slaughtering of the animal), for sure it is Fisq (a sin and disobedience of Allah). And certainly, the Shayatin (devils) do inspire their friends (from mankind) to dispute with you, and if you obey them [by making Al-Maytatah (a dead animal) legal by eating it], then you would indeed be Mushrikun (polytheists) [because they (devils and their friends) made lawful to you to eat that which Allah has made unlawful to eat and you obeyed them by considering it lawful to eat, and by doing so you worshipped them, and to worship others besides Allah is polytheism].

22:34

And for every nation We have appointed religious ceremonies, that they may mention the Name of Allah over the beast of cattle that He has given them for food. And your Ilah (God) is One Ilah (God Allah), so you must submit to Him Alone (in Islam). And (O Muhammad) give glad tidings to the Mukhbitin [those who obey Allah with humility and are humble from among the true believers of Islamic Monotheism].

Perspective:

The Mosaic Law contains commands proscribing the eating of or intermingling of certain foods. Observant Jews in Jesus' day were scrupulous in seeking to abide by these "food laws," as they were part of God's revelation to Israel. Jesus, however, claims the authority to interpret the true purpose of the Law, and in His teaching He makes clear that food items in and of themselves have no power to defile human beings or sever one spiritually from God. True defilement comes from sinful attitudes and actions that find their origin in the human soul (or heart). That His disciples finally understood this startling departure from the Mosaic Law is clear from the statement in Mark 7:19, "In saying this, Jesus declared all foods clean." This response also indicates that Jesus' early disciples acknowledged that His authority overarched even that of the Law, placing Him in a category by Himself among Jews.

Muhammad's teaching on acceptable (*halal*) and forbidden (*haram*) foods parallels that of the Jewish Testament. In fact, the Quran claims that the foods permitted to the "people of the Book" (generally Jews and Christians, but in light of Jesus' teaching above, a specific reference to the Kosher practices of the Jews) are permitted to Muslims, and vice versa (see 5:5). What is clearly forbidden to Muslims is the meat of any animal found dead, or that has been killed by strangling, by a headlong fall, or by a violent blow or goring. Also, no meat is to be eaten over which the name of Allah has not been pronounced during its slaughtering. All pig products are completely forbidden under any circumstance. Muhammad seems to assume that Allah has made these same laws public to every nation in the religious ceremonies which were divinely appointed for them, so that they all have been taught to speak the name of Allah over their animals slaughtered for food (see 22:34). Two caveats are presented in the Quran whereby Muslims may eat forbidden meats without incurring Allah's wrath: if they are constrained by severe hunger alone (i.e., unprompted by the desire to disobey Allah in this matter—see also 2:173); or if they do not know that the meat was prepared incorrectly and so ate in ignorance (see 33:5).

22. Is there any unforgivable sin?

The Bible says:

Mark 3:28–29 (NKJV)

Assuredly, I say to you, all sins will be forgiven the sons of men, and whatever blasphemies they may utter; but he who blasphemes against the Holy Spirit never has forgiveness, but is subject to eternal condemnation.

The Quran says:

4:48, 137

Verily, Allah forgives not that partners should be set up with him in worship, but He forgives except that (anything else) to whom He pleases, and whoever sets up partners with Allah in worship, he has indeed invented a tremendous sin. . . .

Verily, those who believe, then disbelieve, then believe (again), and (again) disbelieve, and go on increasing in disbelief; Allah will not forgive them, nor guide them on the (Right) Way.

47:34

Verily, those who disbelieve, and hinder (men) from the Path of Allah (i.e. Islam); then die while they are disbelievers, Allah will not forgive them.

Perspective:

Jesus teaches that all sins may be forgiven but one: blasphemy against the Holy Spirit. This He calls an "eternal sin." Scholars have debated what exactly this means, but the context clearly indicates that Jewish leaders have accused Jesus of employing the power of Satan to cast a demon out of a man, and Jesus has responded that Satan would not act against himself in opposing the work of a demon. Instead, the power Jesus employed to free the desperate man from the evil spirit was God's Holy Spirit. Blasphemy against the Spirit thus means attributing to the devil the work of God, and vice versa. Presumably the reason it is unforgivable is that one who has so reversed good and evil in his mind is incapable of crying out to the true God for mercy because he is looking in the wrong direction. Such a person has turned his back completely on God and is unwilling to hear any message other than one supporting his perverted view of good and evil.

Muhammad insists that though one cannot be sure that all one's sins will be forgiven by Allah, there is certainly one sin that will never be forgiven by Allah: the sin of *shirk*. Literally, this Arabic word means "association," and in this context speaks of setting up partners as equals with Allah. The creation and worship of idols robs God of His proper glory, and He will punish with hellfire those who persist in this sin. 4:137 and 47:34 underscore the claim that double-minded Muslims who die in unbelief and those who hinder others from the path of Allah will also never be forgiven.

23. How should believers treat those they meet?

The Bible says:

Matthew 7:12 (NIV)
So in everything, do to others what you would have them do to you, for this sums up the Law and the Prophets.

The Quran says:

3:28
Let not the believers take the disbelievers as *Auliya* (supporters, helpers, etc.) instead of the believers, and whoever does that will never be helped by Allah in any way, except if you indeed fear a danger from them. And Allah warns you against Himself (His Punishment), and to Allah is the final return.

5:51
O you who believe! Take not the Jews and the Christians as *Auliya'* (friends, protectors, helpers, etc.), they are but *Auliya'* to one another. And if any amongst you takes them as *Auliya'*, then surely he is one of them. Verily, Allah guides not those people who are the *Zalimun* (polytheists and wrong-doers and unjust).

Perspective:

When Jesus is questioned about the greatest of the commandments, He declares that loving God is our highest priority and value. But, He adds, to love our neighbors as ourselves goes hand in hand with this first command. In the Sermon on the Mount, Jesus teaches what has become known as the Golden Rule: "In everything, do to others what you would have them do to you," and concludes that to live by this precept is to fulfill the Law. The Golden Rule is a practical application of loving our neighbors as ourselves. It calls us to treat everyone we meet as we ourselves would wish to be treated by them. As such, it is truly the law of love.

Muhammad makes a vital distinction between Muslims and those outside his community. While Muslims are to treat one another as family, and to show love and deference to each other, the same rule does not apply to those who have not yet accepted, or who have rejected, Islam. They are to be called to submission, and warned of the consequences of failing to become Muslims, and then fought until they surrender. Though the People of the Book are exempted from forced conversion, nonetheless Muslims are warned not to develop close ties with Christians or Jews. If they do, they will lose their place in the Muslim community and be treated as outsiders along with their friends or protectors (*Auliya*), who according to Muhammad are not rightly guided by God. This is all summed up in 48:29, where we are told, "Those who are with him (i.e., Muhammad) are severe against disbelievers, and merciful among themselves."

24. What is the nature of the devil (Satan)?

The Bible says:

John 8:44–45 (NLT)

You are the children of your father the devil, and you love to do the evil things he does. He was a murderer from the beginning. He has always hated the truth, because there is no truth in him. When he lies, it is consistent with his character; for he is a liar and the father of lies. So when I tell the truth, you just naturally don't believe me!

John 12:31 (NLT)

The time for judging this world has come, when Satan, the ruler of this world, will be cast out.

The Quran says:

18:50

And (remember) when We said to the angels; "Prostrate to Adam." So they prostrated except *Iblis* (Satan). He was one of the jinns; he disobeyed the Command of his Lord. Will you then take him (*Iblis*) and his offspring as protectors and helpers rather than Me while they are enemies to you? What an evil is the exchange for the *Zalimun* (polytheists, and wrong-doers, etc).

15:30–35

So, the angels prostrated themselves, all of them together. Except *Iblis* (Satan),—he refused to be among the prostrators. (Allah) said: "O *Iblis* (Satan)! What is your reason for not being among the prostrators?" [*Iblis* (Satan)] said: "I am not the one to prostrate myself to a human being, whom You created from sounding clay of altered black smooth mud." (Allah) said: "Then, get out from here, for verily, you are *Rajim* (an outcast or a cursed one)." And verily, the curse shall be upon you till the Day of Recompense (i.e. the Day of Resurrection)."

7:12

(Allah) said: "What prevented you (O *Iblis*) that you did not prostrate, when I commanded you?" *Iblis* said: "I am better than him (Adam), You created me from fire, and him You created from clay."

Perspective:

Though Jesus does not address the ontological nature of the devil (it is widely accepted in Christian tradition that he is a fallen archangel), He does speak of the devil's *modus operandi* and of his relationship to the world. It is clear from the temptations Jesus faced in the desert (see Luke 4) that the devil possessed power and authority beyond that of mere mortals. In John 8:44 we read Jesus' declaration that the devil is "a murderer from the beginning" in whom there is no truth. Indeed, he is the father of lies. This seems to point back to the Genesis temptation account (Genesis 3), linking the devil with the serpent, whose lies to Eve led to sin and the divine penalty of death for the human race. Jesus also refers to the devil as the prince of this world (John 12:31; 14:30; 16:11), indicating that this world is presently in the grip of the evil under the usurped authority of the chief evil one, the devil. Christ's coming, however, trumpets the end to the devil's dominion with the arrival of the reign of God inaugurated by Jesus.

The Quran clearly links the devil (*Shaitan*, who is also known as Iblis [Satan]) with the temptation of Adam and Eve in the Garden. His fury against the human race stems from Allah's command for all the angels to bow before Adam at his creation. The devil alone refuses to prostrate himself before Adam, declaring that his nature (fire) was nobler than Adam's (clay). For his arrogance, Allah expels him from Paradise, and in return the devil blames God for having misled him and declares that he will now set about misleading human beings to their destruction. As to the devil's ontological nature, the Quran speaks a bit confusedly of his being both an angel (created of light) and a jinni (creature of fire).

25. What motivates Satan to action?

The Bible says:

Mark 4:15 (ESV)

These are the ones along the path, where the word is sown: when they hear, Satan immediately comes and takes away the word that is sown in them.

Luke 4:1–13 (ESV)

Jesus, full of the Holy Spirit, returned from the Jordan and was led by the Spirit in the wilderness for forty days, being tempted by the devil. And he ate nothing during those days. And when they were ended, he was hungry. The devil said to him, "If you are the Son of God, command this stone to become bread." And Jesus answered him, "It is written, 'Man shall not live by bread alone.'" And the devil took him up and showed him all the kingdoms of the world in a moment of time, and said to him, "To you I will give all this authority and their glory, for it has been delivered to me, and I give it to whom I will. If you, then, will worship me, it will all be yours." And Jesus answered him, "It is written, "'You shall worship the Lord your God, and him only shall you serve.'"

And he took him to Jerusalem and set him on the pinnacle of the temple and said to him, "If you are the Son of God, throw yourself down from here, for it is written, "'He will command his angels concerning you, to guard you,' and "'On their hands they will bear you up, lest you strike your foot against a stone.'"

And Jesus answered him, "It is said, 'You shall not put the Lord your God to the test.'" And when the devil had ended every temptation, he departed from him until an opportune time.

(See also Mark 8:33; Luke 13:16; 22:31.)

The Quran says:

3:155

Those of you who turned back on the day the two hosts met (i.e. the battle of Uhud), it was *Shaitan* (Satan) who caused them to backslide (run away from the battlefield) because of some (sins) they had earned. But Allah, indeed, has forgiven them. Surely, Allah is Oft-Forgiving, Most Forbearing.

4:60, 120

Have you seen those (hyprocrites) who claim that they believe in that which has been sent down to you, and that which was sent down before you, and they wish to go for judgement (in their disputes) to the *Taghut* (false judges, etc.) while they have been ordered to reject them. But *Shaitan* (Satan) wishes to lead them far astray....

He [*Shaitan* (Satan)] makes promises to them, and arouses in them false desires; and *Shaitan's* (Satan) promises are nothing but deceptions.

5:91
Shaitan (Satan) wants only to excite enmity and hatred between you with intoxicants (alcoholic drinks) and gambling, and hinder you from the remembrance of Allah and from *As-Salat* (the prayer). So, will you not then abstain?

7:27
O Children of Adam! Let not *Shaitan* (Satan) deceive you, as he got your parents [Adam and Hawwa (Eve)] out of Paradise, stripping them of their raiments, to show them their private parts. Verily, he and *Qabiluhu* (his soldiers from the jinns or his tribe) see you from where you cannot see them. Verily, We made the *Shayatin* (devils) *Auliya'* (protectors and helpers) for those who believe not.

Perspective:

In Jesus' many references to Satan it is clear that the devil's central goal is to derail God's plans concerning the salvation of human beings. This is seen quintessentially in his temptations of Jesus in the wilderness, seeking to lure Jesus into following a messianic path that would put the Son of God at odds with His Father's will. Likewise it is reflected in Satan's continual attempts to separate human beings from the Word of God so as to keep them in ignorance of the truth. Lastly, in his desire to oppose God's will and demean His glory, Satan does whatever he can to injure, bind and destroy human beings, the apple of God's eye, in an attempt to foil God's purposes and undermine His glory. Whereas Jesus declares His purpose in John 10:10 to bring abundant life to all who will follow Him, he also characterizes Satan and his minions in terms of "the thief [who] comes only to steal and kill and destroy."

According to the Quran as well, Satan (*Shaitan* in Arabic) has been a deceiver from the beginning. His desire is to mislead believers, to promise them what he cannot deliver in an attempt to draw them away from Allah, causing them to backslide from their commitment to fight in the way of Islam. Temptations to gamble and to use intoxicants of all kinds are some of Satan's favorite tricks to hinder human beings from remembering their duty to God, especially the five daily prayers. The devil's hatred of the human race stems from his own pride and refusal to acknowledge the special favor God has bestowed on human beings in commanding His angels to bow before them, something Iblis (the devil) refused to do.

26. What is Satan's ultimate fate?

The Bible says:

Matthew 25:41 (NKJV)
Then He will also say to those on the left hand, "Depart from Me, you cursed, into the everlasting fire prepared for the devil and his angels."

The Quran says:

7:18
(Allah) said (to *Iblis*) "Get out from this (Paradise) disgraced and expelled. Whoever of them (mankind) will follow you, then surely I will fill Hell with you all."

Perspective:

In Jesus' teaching on the fate of the unrighteous at the day of judgment, He pictures the Son of Man on the divine throne separating humanity into two divergent groups, much as a shepherd separates his sheep from goats. The unrighteous, under God's curse of wrath, will be sent "into the eternal fire prepared for the devil and his angels" (Matthew 25:41). Later, in verse 46, "eternal fire" is spoken of as "eternal punishment" and contrasted with eternal life. It is possible that Jesus means to say that this fate was always intended for the devil and his angels, as it was "prepared" for them, but was not God's intended desire for human beings until they joined in the same unrighteousness that characterizes Satan and all his followers among the angels. This teaching comports well with the imagery of Revelation 20 where the devil and his agents and all whose names are not "found written in the book of life" (20:15) are thrown into the lake of fire, which is also called "the second death" (20:14).

Muhammad speaks of Satan's rebellion against God in his prideful refusal to obey God's command to kneel before Adam. When God expels Satan from Paradise, the devil reveals his spiteful intention to conspire against the human race so as to deceive them from the straight path—i.e., the religion of Islam. God's final word to Satan in this exchange is that hell is the fate that awaits him and all who choose to follow him. Disgraced and expelled from Paradise forever, all they have to look forward to is an eternity of torture and torment.

27. What role should the Law of God play in our lives?

The Bible says:

Matthew 5:17–20 (NIV)

Do not think that I have come to abolish the Law or the Prophets; I have not come to abolish them but to fulfill them. For truly I tell you, until heaven and earth disappear, not the smallest letter, not the least stroke of a pen, will by any means disappear from the Law until everything is accomplished. Therefore anyone who sets aside one of the least of these commands and teaches others accordingly will be called least in the kingdom of heaven, but whoever practices and teaches these commands will be called great in the kingdom of heaven. For I tell you that unless your righteousness surpasses that of the Pharisees and the teachers of the law, you will certainly not enter the kingdom of heaven.

Mark 10:17–21 (NIV)

As Jesus started on his way, a man ran up to him and fell on his knees before him. "Good teacher," he asked, "what must I do to inherit eternal life?"

"Why do you call me good?" Jesus answered. "No one is good—except God alone. You know the commandments: 'You shall not murder, you shall not commit adultery, you shall not steal, you shall not give false testimony, you shall not defraud, honor your father and mother.'"

"Teacher," he declared, "all these I have kept since I was a boy."

Jesus looked at him and loved him. "One thing you lack," he said. "Go, sell everything you have and give to the poor, and you will have treasure in heaven. Then come, follow me."

The Quran says:

3:50

And I have come confirming that which was before me of the Taurat (Torah), and to make lawful to you part of what was forbidden to you, and I have come to you with a proof from your Lord. So fear Allah and obey me.

5:48

And We have sent down to you (O Muhammad) the Book (this Qur'an) in truth, confirming the Scripture that came before it and *Mohayminan* (trustworthy in highness and a witness) over it (old Scriptures). So judge between them by what Allah has revealed, and follow not their vain desires, diverging away from the truth that has come to you. To each among you, We have prescribed a law and a clear way. . . .

4:136

O you who believe! Believe in Allah, and His Messenger (Muhammad), and the Book (the Qur'an) which He has sent down to His Messenger, and the Scripture which He sent down to those before (him), and whosoever disbelieves in Allah, His Angels, His Books, His Messengers, and the Last Day, then indeed he has strayed far away.

46:12
And before this was the Scripture of Musa (Moses) as a guide and a mercy. And this is a confirming Book (the Qur'an) in the Arabic language, to warn those who do wrong, and as glad tidings to the *Muhsinun* (good-doers—see V.2:112).

Perspective:

Jesus makes it clear in His ministry that the Law of God is meant to be obeyed. As to His own role, Jesus claims that His divine purpose was not to eradicate the Law but to obey it fully and so to demonstrate what perfect human life before God was meant to look like. Unlike the religious leaders of His day, who looked for loopholes even while appearing to be rigorously righteous, Jesus uncompromisingly declared that the laws of God must not be compromised or evaded.

From His Sermon on the Mount teachings we learn that outward obedience to the letter of the Law is insufficient; one must embrace the spirit of the Law as well in one's attitudes and motives. Hence, when a rich, religious man sought out Jesus seeking to know how to "inherit eternal life" (Mark 10:17) and Jesus pointed him to the Law (abbreviated in the form of the Ten Commandments), the religious man replied confidently that he had been keeping these laws ever since he was a boy (i.e., from the time of his bar mitzvah, when he became a "son of the commandment"). Jesus reveals the poverty of this man's grasp of obedience to the Law when he invites the man to donate all of his riches to the poor in order that he might receive "treasure in heaven" (10:21). The wealthy man's refusal to give up his riches at that point demonstrated the idolatry of his heart in placing material things before God in importance.

Muhammad affirms in 3:50 that Jesus came to confirm the Law revealed through Moses, but also to "make lawful part of what had been forbidden to you." In this, Jesus wields greater authority than even the Taurat (the Torah). The Quran in turn has been given to the world through Muhammad to confirm the prior revelations of God through all His prophets. It is meant for total obedience by the whole human race. One's eternal reward or punishment will depend (generally) on how well or poorly one obeys the commands of the Quran, expanded in the first three centuries of Islam to become the corpus now known as *sharia*. While in Jesus' teachings the Law points us to a relationship of responsive love toward God, in Islam the Law is the unbreakable will of God to which each human heart must submit.

28. Who is God's final messenger to the world?

The Bible says:

John 3:16 (NLT)

For God loved the world so much that he gave his one and only Son, so that everyone who believes in him will not perish but have eternal life.

Matthew 28:18–20 (NLT)

Jesus came and told his disciples, "I have been given all authority in heaven and on earth. Therefore, go and make disciples of all the nations, baptizing them in the name of the Father and the Son and the Holy Spirit. Teach these new disciples to obey all the commands I have given you. And be sure of this: I am with you always, even to the end of the age."

The Quran says:

25:1

Blessed be He Who sent down the criterion (of right and wrong, i.e. this Qur'an) to His slave (Muhammad) that he may be a warner to the 'Alamin (mankind and jinns).

3:20

So if they dispute with you (Muhammad) say: "I have submitted myself to Allah (in Islam), and (so have) those who follow me." And say to those who were given the Scripture (Jews and Christians) and to those who are illiterates (Arab pagans): "Do you (also) submit yourselves (to Allah in Islam)?" If they do, they are rightly guided; but if they turn away, your duty is only to convey the Message; and Allah is All-Seer of (His) slaves.

33:40

Muhammad is not the father of any man among you, but he is the Messenger of Allah and the last (end) of the Prophets. And Allah is Ever All-Aware of everything.

Perspective:

*J*esus makes clear His belief that He is God's only begotten Son, who from eternity has been next to the heart of His Father in heaven (see John 1:18), and so is uniquely qualified to share with the world God's ultimate revelation.

The culmination of God's love for the human race is seen in the gift of His Son sent to sacrifice Himself for the salvation of lost sinners. In His last post-resurrection appearance to the disciples recorded in Matthew 28:18–20, Jesus claims that the Father has granted to Him all authority in heaven and earth. There is no being whose message can stand in rivalry with that of Jesus. All human beings are therefore called to become His followers, and the disciples are to go to every nation spreading this message. Jesus is God's final messenger to the world. The opening of the letter to the Hebrews sums this up succinctly: "In the past God spoke to our ancestors through the prophets at many times and in various ways, but in these last days he has spoken to us by his Son, whom he appointed heir of all things, and through whom also he made the universe" (Hebrews 1:1–2).

The Quran, on the other hand, sees Jesus as one among a long line of prophets whom God has sent over human history to various lands and peoples. Jesus was sent primarily to the Jews, and His message paralleled that of every other prophet before Him. Muhammad, on the other hand, is the last of the prophets, sent by God to all mankind, according to 33:40. To him has been given the final revelation of the Quran, which is the ultimate criterion of right and wrong (25:1) by which Muhammad is to warn all creation of God's coming judgment and call to obedience. Since the Quran is the pinnacle of God's revelation, there can be no more prophets after him, and certainly no prior prophet's words can upstage those of Muhammad.

29. What is primary among the responsibilities of believers?

The Bible says:

Acts 1:8 (ESV)

But you will receive power when the Holy Spirit has come upon you, and you will be my witnesses in Jerusalem and in all Judea and Samaria, and to the end of the earth.

The Quran says:

2:143

Thus We have made you [true Muslims—real believers of Islamic Monotheism, true followers of Prophet Muhammad and his *Sunnah* (legal ways)], a *Wasat* (just) (and the best) nation, that you be witnesses over mankind and the Messenger (Muhammad) be a witness over you. And We made the *Qiblah* (prayer direction towards Jerusalem) which you used to face, only to test those who followed the Messenger (Muhammad) from those who would turn on their heels (i.e. disobey the Messenger). Indeed it was great (heavy) except for those whom Allah guided. And Allah would never make your faith (prayers) to be lost (i.e. your prayers offered towards Jerusalem). Truly, Allah is full of kindness, the Most Merciful towards mankind.

Perspective:

*J*ust prior to His ascension to heaven, Jesus directs His followers to wait together in Jerusalem (Acts 1:8). Why? Because God will pour out His Holy Spirit upon them, granting them power for their primary responsibility—to be witnesses to all the world of the life, death and resurrection of Jesus Christ, so that all may come to know Him as Savior and Lord and so become His disciples. The rest of the book of Acts tracks the efforts of Jesus' first disciples and subsequent converts to carry out this responsibility of bearing witness to Jesus before all the inhabited Roman Empire. His disciples since then have carried that same gospel message to the world.

According to the Quran (2:143), Muslims are also called to be witnesses to all the world of the oneness of God (i.e., that there is only one God, creator of all and the judge to whom all human beings will one day answer), and of the role of Muhammad as God's final messenger to the whole human race. As Muhammad served as a warner of his hearers, so all Muslims are to follow in his footsteps and bear witness to Islam by warning all with whom they come into contact that they should submit to God and become Muslims as well.

30. How did Jesus and Muhammad refer to each other in their respective teachings?

The Bible says:

Mark 12:1–11 (ESV)

And he began to speak to them in parables. "A man planted a vineyard and put a fence around it and dug a pit for the winepress and built a tower, and leased it to tenants and went into another country. When the season came, he sent a servant to the tenants to get from them some of the fruit of the vineyard. And they took him and beat him and sent him away empty-handed. Again he sent to them another servant, and they struck him on the head and treated him shamefully. And he sent another, and him they killed. And so with many others: some they beat, and some they killed. He had still one other, a beloved son. Finally he sent him to them, saying, 'They will respect my son.' But those tenants said to one another, 'This is the heir. Come, let us kill him, and the inheritance will be ours.' And they took him and killed him and threw him out of the vineyard. What will the owner of the vineyard do? He will come and destroy the tenants and give the vineyard to others. Have you not read this Scripture: "'The stone that the builders rejected has become the cornerstone; this was the Lord's doing, and it is marvelous in our eyes'?"

Hebrews 1:1–2 (ESV)

Long ago, at many times and in many ways, God spoke to our fathers by the prophets, but in these last days he has spoken to us by his Son, whom he appointed the heir of all things, through whom also he created the world.

The Quran says:

3:45, 48–49

(Remember) when the angels said: "O Maryam (Mary)! Verily, Allah gives you the glad tidings of a Word from Him, his name will be the Messiah 'Isa (Jesus), the son of Maryam (Mary), held in honour in this world and in the Hereafter, and will be one of those who are near to Allah.". . . And He (Allah) will teach him the Book and Al-Hikmah, the Taurat (Torah) and the Injeel (Gospel). And will make him a Messenger to the Children of Israel (saying): "I have come to you with a sign from your Lord, that I design for you out of clay, as it were, the figure of a bird, and breathe into it, and it becomes a bird by Allah's Leave; and I heal him who was born blind, and the leper, and I bring the dead to life by Allah's Leave.

4:171

O people of the Scripture (Jews and Christians)! Do not exceed the limits in your religion, nor say of Allah aught but the truth. The Messiah 'Isa (Jesus), son of Maryam (Mary), was (no more than) a Messenger of Allah and His Word, which He bestowed on Maryam (Mary) and a spirit (Ruh) from Him; so believe in Allah and His Messengers. Say not: "Three (trinity)!"

Cease! (it is) better for you. For Allah is (the only) One Ilah (God), Glory be to Him (Far Exalted is He) above having a son. To Him belongs all that is in the heavens and all that is in the earth. And Allah is All-Sufficient as a Disposer of affairs.

Perspective:

Since Jesus lived and died over five hundred years before Muhammad's birth, the only way He might have referred to Muhammad would have been through prophecy. Nothing in orthodox New Testament scholarship would lend any credence to claims by Muslims that Jesus Himself or any of His apostolic followers pointed forward to a prophet yet to come who would supersede Jesus. (See Question 53 for discussion of whether Jesus' teaching about the "Advocate" that He would send to the disciples after His own ascension refers to the Holy Spirit or to Muhammad.)

Further, the fact that Jesus understood Himself to be the fulfillment of God's promises to the world logically implies that there is no other major figure to come in God's plans for the world. In Jesus' parable of the wicked tenants (Mark 12:1–12), the son of the owner represents Jesus, of course, indicating His self-assessment that He stands alone from the prophets as an only son stands separate from the servants in his father's house. As the author of the epistle to the Hebrews says (1:1–2), in the past God had sent prophets to His people, but now He has spoken fully through His Son. After the Son has come, the appearance of any further servants (prophets) would be superfluous. In light of these truths, it is inconceivable that Jesus would have hinted about the coming of any future prophet, including Muhammad. In fact, Jesus warns His followers that false messiahs and false prophets will arise to seek to mislead people before the end, but there will be no more divinely appointed leaders until the Son of Man returns at the end of the age.

On the other hand, Muhammad referred often to Jesus ('Isa) in the Quran, applying to him unique and extraordinary titles. Jesus is not only a major prophet or apostle of God, He is the Messiah, a Word from God/Word of truth, a spirit sent from Him, one who is faultless. Muhammad most often refers to Jesus as the son of Mary, an acknowledgement that Jesus was virgin born and so had no earthly father. No other man sent from God is credited with the kind of miracles Muhammad attributes to Jesus: healing the blind and lame, cleansing lepers, raising the dead. Nevertheless, he rejects that Jesus is any more than a servant of Allah; He cannot be the Son of God, Savior or Lord. He is not to be worshiped or given equal stature with God.

31. How are we to share our faith with others?

The Bible says:

Luke 9:1–5 (NIV)

When Jesus had called the Twelve together, he gave them power and authority to drive out all demons and to cure diseases, and he sent them out to proclaim the kingdom of God and to heal the sick. He told them: "Take nothing for the journey—no staff, no bag, no bread, no money, no extra shirt. Whatever house you enter, stay there until you leave that town. If people do not welcome you, leave their town and shake the dust off your feet as a testimony against them."

The Quran says:

16:125

Invite (mankind, O Muhammad) to the Way of your Lord (i.e. Islam) with wisdom (i.e. with the Divine Inspiration and the Qur'an) and fair preaching, and argue with them in a way that is better. Truly, your Lord knows best who has gone astray from His Path, and He is the Best Aware of those who are guided.

29:46

And argue not with the people of the Scripture (Jews and Christians), unless it be in (a way) that is better (with good words and in good manner, inviting them to Islamic Monotheism with His Verses), except with such of them as do wrong, and say (to them): "We believe in that which has been revealed to us and revealed to you; our *Ilah* (God) and your *Ilah* (God) is One (i.e. Allah), and to Him we have submitted (as Muslims)."

Perspective:

Jesus commissions His disciples to share the good news of God's advancing victory over the powers of darkness. They are sent out two by two into towns and villages to declare God's welcoming love by their messages and by their actions. So they point people to Jesus as God's promised Savior, and under His authority they heal all manner of diseases and cast out demons to drive home the truth that God indeed is reclaiming His world from Satan's evil usurpation, and is welcoming all the oppressed and hurting into His Kingdom of righteousness and love. So today, Jesus' followers are to point people to new life available through a personal relationship with God's Son, and under His authority to pray and do good to others in Christ's name.

Allah commands Muhammad to engage in winsome apologetics with all his listeners, inviting them to the straight path of Islam. His preaching ought to be persuasive, seeking to convince pagans and even the people of the Book (Jews and Christians) that there is only one God, and that He has given His final words of revelation to the world through Muhammad alone.

With regard to the People of the Book, however, Muhammad and his followers are not to engage in disputation, except with those whose lifestyles show they are not following the ways of God. Muhammad believed that his teachings were fully in accord with the messages that all the prophets before him (including Moses and Jesus) had proclaimed. It is not until the last decade of Muhammad's life that he comes to see that devout Christians and Jews actually held convictions that differed significantly from his, and as his own earthly power increases he employs it as needed to force these groups as well as the many pagan tribes throughout Arabia to submit to Islam and his prophethood, or face enslavement or death instead.

32. Are we to use force to overcome those who oppose God?

The Bible says:

JOHN 18:36 (NKJV)

Jesus answered, "My kingdom is not of this world. If My kingdom were of this world, My servants would fight, so that I should not be delivered to the Jews; but now My kingdom is not from here."

Matthew 26:51–54 (NKJV)

Suddenly, one of those who were with Jesus stretched out his hand and drew his sword, struck the servant of the high priest, and cut off his ear.

But Jesus said to him, "Put your sword in its place, for all who take the sword will perish by the sword. Or do you think that I cannot now pray to My Father, and He will provide Me with more than twelve legions of angels? How then could the Scriptures be fulfilled, that it must happen thus?"

The Quran says:

9:5, 29

Then when the Sacred Months have passed, then kill the *Mushrikun* wherever you find them, and capture them and besiege them, and prepare for them each and every ambush. But if they repent and perform *As-Salat*, and give *Zakat*, then leave their way free. Verily, Allah is Oft-Forgiving, Most Merciful....

Fight against those who believe not in Allah, nor in the Last Day, nor forbid that which has been forbidden by Allah and His Messenger and those who acknowledge not the religion of truth (i.e. Islam) among the people of the Scripture (Jews and Christians), until they pay the *Jizyah* with willing submission, and feel themselves subdued.

2:190–192

And fight in the Way of Allah those who fight you, but transgress not the limits. Truly, Allah likes not the transgressors. And kill them wherever you find them, and turn them out from where they have turned you out. And *Al-Fitnah* is worse than killing. And fight not with them at *Al-Masjid-al-Haram* (the sanctuary at Makkah), unless they fight you there. But if they attack you, then kill them. Such is the recompense of the disbelievers. But if they cease, then Allah is Oft-Forgiving, Most Merciful.

47:4

So, when you meet those who disbelieve smite at their necks till when you have killed and wounded many of them, then bind a bond firmly (on them, i.e. take them as captives).

2:216

Jihad (holy fighting in Allah's Cause) is ordained for you (Muslims) though you dislike it....

Perspective:

Jesus eschews the use of force or violence in the advancement of the Kingdom of God. Since His rule is not like that of earthly kings, and His authority over others is not like that of earthly politicians, Jesus calls for a voluntary and joyful submission to His Lordship. In His discussion with Pontius Pilate (a Roman political official who ostensibly held Jesus' life in his hands) about whether Jesus should rightly be called "King of the Jews," Jesus acknowledges His status as king, but claims that His Kingdom is of a different kind than those produced by human strivings. As such, He said, His followers would not rise up to fight against His arrest and execution by worldly authorities. When in fact Jesus is arrested, one of His disciples (identified in John 18:10 as Peter) draws his sword and attacks a man in the crowd. Jesus commands him to put away the sword, declaring that all who live by the sword will die by the sword. His kingdom is not to be built upon force and violence. Indeed, He claims, should He wish to be defended from His opponents, He only need call upon His heavenly Father, and immediately twelve legions of angels would be placed at His disposal to protect Him. In Roman parlance a legion of soldiers numbered six thousand. Seventy-two thousand angels would be a deterrent by anyone's standards. Yet Jesus refuses to employ brute force to institute His will, and He forbids His followers from doing so in His name.

According to the Quran, Allah progressively revealed to Muhammad and his followers that they were justified in using the sword in the advancement of Islam. First, they were granted permission to employ force in self-defense. Later, the use of aggressive force in imposing Islam on new peoples or territories was commanded. Known as *jihad* (lit: "striving"), this term is linked repeatedly in the Quran with the term *qital* (lit: "battle, warfare") and demonstrates that *jihad* (though it can carry peaceful meanings) becomes a technical term in Islam to indicate armed fighting to advance the cause of Islam.

Some say that these revelations were given early to Muhammad, but then later abrogated by verses enjoining peace and tolerance. But three truths argue against such a revisionist view of Islam: first, the early Muslim biographies of Muhammad and his followers demonstrate that the prophet and his armies were committed to expansion by force when necessary throughout his whole life; second, orthodox Muslim scholarship has asserted from its inception that the verses commanding *jihad* by the sword abrogate the verses enjoining peace and tolerance, not the other way around; third, the history of Islam in its first hundred plus years reflects the community's understanding that advancement of Islam by force was indeed the will of God as revealed in the Quran through their prophet.

33. How can we find peace with God?

The Bible says:

John 14:27 (NLT)

I am leaving you with a gift—peace of mind and heart. And the peace I give is a gift the world cannot give. So don't be troubled or afraid.

John 16:32–33 (NLT)

The time is coming—indeed it's here now—when you will be scattered, each one going his own way, leaving me alone. Yet I am not alone because the Father is with me. I have told you all this so that you may have peace in me. Here on earth you will have many trials and sorrows. But take heart, because I have overcome the world.

The Quran says:

5:15–16

O people of the Scripture (Jews and Christians)! Now has come to you Our Messenger (Muhammad) explaining to you much of that which you used to hide from the Scripture and passing over (i.e. leaving out without explaining) much. Indeed, there has come to you from Allah a light (Prophet Muhammad) and a plain Book (this Qur'an). Wherewith Allah guides all those who seek His Good Pleasure to ways of peace, and He brings them out of darkness by His Will unto light and guides them to a Straight Way (Islamic Monotheism).

6:125–127

And whomsoever Allah wills to guide, He opens his breast to Islam, and whomsoever He wills to send astray, He makes his breast closed and constricted, as if he is climbing up to the sky. Thus Allah puts the wrath on those who believe not. And this is the Path of your Lord (the Qur'an and Islam) leading Straight. We have detailed Our Revelations for a people who take heed. For them will be the home of peace (Paradise) with their Lord. And He will be their Wali (Helper and Protector) because of what they used to do.

10:25–27

Allah calls to the home of peace (i.e. Paradise, by accepting Allah's religion of Islamic Monotheism and by doing righteous good deeds and abstaining from polytheism and evil deeds) and guides whom He wills to a Straight Path. For those who have done good is the best (reward, i.e. Paradise) and even more (i.e. having the honour of glancing at the Countenance of Allah) Neither darkness nor dust nor any humiliating disgrace shall cover their faces. They are the dwellers of Paradise, they will abide therein forever. And those who have earned evil deeds, the recompense of an evil deed is the like thereof, and humiliating disgrace will cover them (their faces). No defender will they have from Allah. Their faces will be covered, as it were, with pieces from the darkness of night. They are dwellers of the Fire, they will abide therein forever.

Perspective:

This question assumes that by nature we do not have peace with God already, but are alienated from Him for some reason. One of the principal themes of the Bible is that our disobedience to God has fractured our relationship with God and we are helpless to repair that breach. The message of the gospel is that God Himself has taken the initiative to heal that rift by sending His only Son to bring reconciliation and redemption to a lost humanity by His own self-sacrifice. Jesus, in speaking to His disciples, teaches them that if they will abide with Him and allow Him to live within them by His Spirit, He will give them His peace, a peace that the world cannot understand or give itself. This is the peace that reestablishes life with God, and places the believer in the heart of God's love and purposes.

It is Allah who brings peace to those whose hearts He guides to the "straight path" of Islam. Such individuals, who demonstrate by their obedience to all His laws their submission to His will, and overflow with good works, will be granted access to abode of peace, i.e., to Paradise. They will be forever safe from His wrath, while those whose hearts remain closed to Islam (by Allah's decree) will receive only eternal wrath from Him and never know peace.

34. What is heaven like?

The Bible says:

Luke 20:34–36 (NKJV)

Jesus answered and said to them, "The sons of this age marry and are given in marriage. But those who are counted worthy to attain that age, and the resurrection from the dead, neither marry nor are given in marriage; nor can they die anymore, for they are equal to the angels and are sons of God, being sons of the resurrection."

John 14:2–3 (NKJV)

In My Father's house are many mansions; if it were not so, I would have told you. I go to prepare a place for you. And if I go and prepare a place for you, I will come again and receive you to Myself; that where I am, there you may be also.

Matthew 25:31–40 (NKJV)

When the Son of Man comes in His glory, and all the holy angels with Him, then He will sit on the throne of His glory. All the nations will be gathered before Him, and He will separate them one from another, as a shepherd divides his sheep from the goats. And He will set the sheep on His right hand, but the goats on the left. Then the King will say to those on His right hand, "Come, you blessed of My Father, inherit the kingdom prepared for you from the foundation of the world: for I was hungry and you gave Me food; I was thirsty and you gave Me drink; I was a stranger and you took Me in; I was naked and you clothed Me; I was sick and you visited Me; I was in prison and you came to Me." . . . Assuredly, I say to you, inasmuch as you did it to one of the least of these My brethren, you did it to Me.

The Quran says:

56:28–37

(The pious will be) among thornless lote-trees, Among *Talh* (banana-trees) with fruits piled one above another, In shade long-extended, By water flowing constantly, And fruit in plenty, Whose season is not limited, and their supply will not be cut off, And on couches or thrones, raised high. Verily, We have created them (maidens) of special creation. And made them virgins. Loving (their husbands only), equal in age.

36:55–58

Verily, the dwellers of the Paradise, that Day, will be busy in joyful things. They and their wives will be in pleasant shade, reclining on thrones. They will have therein fruits (of all kinds) and all that they ask for. . . .

78:31–37

Verily, for the *Muttaqun*, there will be a success (Paradise); Gardens and grapeyards; And young full-breasted (mature) maidens of equal age; And a full cup (of wine). No *Laghw* (dirty, false, evil talk) shall they hear therein, nor lying; A reward from your Lord, an ample calculated gift.

(From) the Lord of the heavens and the earth, and whatsoever is in between them, the Most Beneficent, none can dare to speak with Him.

47:15
The description of Paradise which the *Muttaqun* (pious) have been promised is that in it are rivers of water the taste and smell of which are not changed; rivers of milk of which the taste never changes; rivers of wine delicious to those who drink; and rivers of clarified honey (clear and pure) therein for them is every kind of fruit; and forgiveness from their Lord....

Perspective:

Jesus gave very little in the way of descriptors concerning the "geography" of heaven. He uses terms like "inheritance," "reward," "treasure," "rooms." Though He never defines these, the context makes it clear that heaven is a destination to be deeply desired. Jesus seems more concerned with identifying the qualities of life and relationship which characterize existence in heaven than with physical or material attributes. We are told that in the age of resurrection God's people will not be married, but like the angels will be completely free to serve God wholly. Their character will be that of Jesus Himself, represented well by the beatitudes and subsequent teaching in the Sermon on the Mount (Matthew 5—7), as well as by the love and compassion evidenced in the parable of the sheep and goats (Matthew 25). But the overall emphasis is one of relationship to Jesus as Lord and to God as Father. Believers will dwell at home with the Father, and Jesus Himself will prepare the way and bring them there that they may be with Him forever in the presence of His and their Father.

The Quran knows no such reticence in speaking graphically about the makeup of heaven. It will be a place of temperate seasons, with abundant orchards, gardens and vineyards watered by numberless streams of pure water, of milk, of honey and of wine. Believers and their wives will recline in peace and joy on thrones in cool shade. Young lads will hover to serve them, and for the men there will be *houris*—young, full-breasted women created specifically in heaven for them, who have eyes only for their men, who never tire of sexual relations and yet always retain their virginity (a highly prized quality for Muslim brides). Heaven is reserved for those forgiven by Allah. It is a place of sensual pleasures for eternity, but God is not present there. His abode is above heaven, for He is too lofty and majestic to make His dwelling with humans, even those who have served Him faithfully.

35. What is hell like?

The Bible says:

Matthew 13:40–42 (ESV)

Just as the weeds are gathered and burned with fire, so will it be at the end of the age. The Son of Man will send his angels, and they will gather out of his kingdom all causes of sin and all law-breakers, and throw them into the fiery furnace. In that place there will be weeping and gnashing of teeth.

Mark 9:43–48 (ESV)

If your hand causes you to sin, cut it off. It is better for you to enter life crippled than with two hands to go to hell, to the unquenchable fire. And if your foot causes you to sin, cut it off. It is better for you to enter life lame than with two feet to be thrown into hell. And if your eye causes you to sin, tear it out. It is better for you to enter the kingdom of God with one eye than with two eyes to be thrown into hell, "where their worm does not die and the fire is not quenched."

The Quran says:

4:56

Surely! Those who disbelieved in Our *Ayat* (proofs, evidences, verses) We shall burn them in Fire. As often as their skins are roasted through, We shall change them for other skins that they may taste the punishment. Truly, Allah is Ever Most Powerful, All-Wise.

9:34–35

O you who believe! Verily, there are many of the (Jewish) rabbis and the (Christian) monks who devour the wealth of mankind in falsehood, and hinder (them) from the Way of Allah (i.e. Allah's Religion of Islamic Monotheism). And those who hoard up gold and silver [*Al-Kanz*: the money, the *Zakat* of which has not been paid], and spend it not in the Way of Allah, -announce unto them a painful torment. On the Day when that (*Al-Kanz*: money, gold and silver, etc., the *Zakat* of which has not been paid) will be heated in the Fire of Hell and with it will be branded their foreheads, their flanks, and their backs, (and it will be said unto them):- "This is the treasure which you hoarded for yourselves. Now taste of what you used to hoard."

14:16–17

In front of him (every obstinate, arrogant dictator) is Hell, and he will be made to drink boiling, festering water. He will sip it unwillingly, and he will find a great difficulty to swallow it down his throat , and death will come to him from every side, yet he will not die and in front of him, will be a great torment....

18:29

... Verily, We have prepared for the *Zalimun* (polytheists and wrong-doers, etc.), a Fire whose walls will be surrounding them. And if they ask for help (relief, water, etc.) they will be granted water like boiling oil, that will scald their faces. Terrible the drink, and an evil *Murtafaqa* (dwelling, resting place, etc.)!

22:19-22

... then as for those who disbelieve, garments of fire will be cut out for them, boiling water will be poured down over their heads. With it will melt or vanish away what is within their bellies, as well as (their) skins. And for them are hooked rods of iron (to punish them). Every time they seek to get away therefrom, from anguish, they will be driven back therein, and (it will be) said to them: "Taste the torment of burning!"

44:43-49

Verily, the tree of *Zaqqum*, Will be the food of the sinners, Like boiling oil, it will boil in the bellies, Like the boiling of scalding water. (It will be said) "Seize him and drag him into the midst of blazing Fire, Then pour over his head the torment of boiling water, Taste you (this)! Verily, you were (pretending to be) the mighty, the generous!

Perspective:

Jesus is more descriptive in His statements on hell than on heaven. Hell is existence outside the Kingdom of God, variously described as outer darkness, unquenchable fire as in a blazing furnace, eternal punishment. It is characterized by weeping and gnashing of teeth, of sorrow and pain. There is good reason to believe that Jesus is speaking in metaphors about a place of true horror and eternal destruction, whose reality surpasses what earthly experiences and human language can adequately capture. Hell's purpose is banishment and punishment of those under God's enduring wrath.

If Jesus' descriptions of hell may be characterized as clear, those from Muhammad might be termed "high definition." We are told in the Quran that the inhabitants of hell will be surrounded by walls of fire, that they will be clad in garments of fire (or burning pitch), have scalding, festering water poured over their heads and down their throats, causing their skin and intestines to melt. Their only food will be from a thorny, poisonous plant, but this will not abate their hunger. Iron hooks will pierce their bodies, and when they try to escape from their anguish they will be driven back amid the cry, "Taste the torment of burning!" Death will draw near to them on every side, yet they will remain alive in their torment forever. Allah declares that as often as their skin is roasted through, He will replace it with new skin so that they may experience the fullness of torment unendingly. Those who hoarded money that should have been donated to Allah will find those same metal coins superheated and applied to their foreheads, flanks and backs in branding fashion with the taunt, "Now taste of what you used to hoard!" Such graphic depictions are no doubt intended to impress upon all listeners that obedience to Allah and His prophet, no matter how difficult or costly, is much preferable to the alternative.

36. What was the purpose of Jesus' crucifixion?

The Bible says:

John 12:31–33 (NIV)

"Now is the time for judgment on this world; now the prince of this world will be driven out. And I, when I am lifted up from the earth, will draw all people to myself." He said this to show the kind of death he was going to die.

Mark 10:45 (NIV)

For even the Son of Man did not come to be served, but to serve, and to give his life as a ransom for many.

Luke 18:31–33 (NIV)

Jesus took the Twelve aside and told them, "We are going up to Jerusalem, and everything that is written by the prophets about the Son of Man will be fulfilled. He will be delivered over to the Gentiles. They will mock him, insult him and spit on him; they will flog him and kill him. On the third day he will rise again."

The Quran says:

4:157–158

And because of their saying (in boast), "We killed Messiah 'Isa (Jesus), son of Maryam (Mary), the Messenger of Allah,"—but they killed him not, nor crucified him, but the resemblance of 'Isa (Jesus) was put over another man (and they killed that man), and those who differ therein are full of doubts. They have no (certain) knowledge, they follow nothing but conjecture. For surely; they killed him not [i.e. 'Isa (Jesus), son of Maryam (Mary)]: But Allah raised him ['Isa (Jesus)] up (with his body and soul) unto Himself (and he is in the heavens). And Allah is Ever All-Powerful, All-Wise.

19:33–34

And *Salam* (peace) be upon me the day I was born, and the day I die, and the day I shall be raised alive!" Such is 'Isa (Jesus), son of Maryam (Mary). (it is) a statement of truth, about which they doubt (or dispute).

3:55

And (remember) when Allah said: "O 'Isa (Jesus)! I will take you and raise you to Myself and clear you [of the forged statement that 'Isa (Jesus) is Allah's son] of those who disbelieve, and I will make those who follow you (Monotheists, who worship none but Allah) superior to those who disbelieve [in the Oneness of Allah, or disbelieve in some of His Messengers, e.g. Muhammad ,'Isa (Jesus), Musa (Moses), etc., or in His Holy Books, e.g. the Taurat (Torah), the Injeel (Gospel), the Qur'an] till the Day of Resurrection. Then you will return to Me and I will judge between you in the matters in which you used to dispute."

Perspective:

Jesus views His impending death as a voluntary sacrifice fulfilling all Old Testament prophecies about the role of the Son of Man (the Messiah). Although his inherent status is exalted, he has not come to be served, but to serve humanity, giving his life as a ransom for those who will believe in Him. According to John 12, Jesus knew in advance the type of death He would suffer, speaking of His body being lifted up from the earth (on a Roman cross). In his prophecy about "draw[ing] all people" to Himself (John 12:32) Jesus clearly sees His death as having universal significance. In speaking of His death as a ransom, He clearly views His sacrifice in substitutionary terms, serving as an atonement for the sins of the world so that those trusting in Him would be spared the death their sins otherwise deserve.

According to the Quran, Jesus himself never suffered crucifixion, though it appeared to His enemies (the Jews) that they had killed Him. There is much speculation as to how this could have happened, but the bottom line is that God rescued His servant Jesus from those out for His blood by raising Him to heaven alive. Most Muslims believe that from the time of His departure from earth, Jesus has been alive in heaven (either conscious or in a state of suspended animation, scheduled to return to earth and live out the rest of His life when God so commands Him. This is the only way to harmonize 4:157–58 with what the infant Jesus is supposed to have said to the crowd gathered to castigate his mother Mary for giving birth to Jesus out of wedlock: "Peace be upon me the day I was born, the day I die, and the day I shall be raised alive." If Jesus did not die on the cross but was "raptured" to heaven, He must return to earth to live out the rest of His natural days and then die so that He may finally be resurrected with the rest of humanity, and so fulfill this prophecy.

Since Muslims deny Jesus' death, they must deny His role as Savior, the sacrificial Lamb of God who takes away the sin of the world, to use the phrasing of John the Baptist in John 1:29. Here is one of the irreconcilable differences between the message of orthodox Islam and that of orthodox Christianity.

37. How do angels serve God?

The Bible says:

Matthew 13:38–42 (NLT)

The field is the world, and the good seed represents the people of the Kingdom. The weeds are the people who belong to the evil one. The enemy who planted the weeds among the wheat is the devil. The harvest is the end of the world, and the harvesters are the angels.

Just as the weeds are sorted out and burned in the fire, so it will be at the end of the world. The Son of Man will send his angels, and they will remove from his Kingdom everything that causes sin and all who do evil. And the angels will throw them into the fiery furnace, where there will be weeping and gnashing of teeth.

Matthew 26:53 (NLT)

Don't you realize that I could ask my Father for thousands of angels to protect us, and he would send them instantly?

Mark 13:27 (NLT)

He will send out his angels to gather his chosen ones from all over the world—from the farthest ends of the earth and heaven.

The Quran says:

82:10–12

But verily, over you (are appointed angels in charge of mankind) to watch you, *Kiraman* (honourable) *Katibin* writing down (your deeds), They know all that you do.

74:31

And We have set none but angels as guardians of the Fire, and We have fixed their number (19) only as a trial for the disbelievers, in order that the people of the Scripture (Jews and Christians) may arrive at a certainty [that this Qur'an is the truth as it agrees with their Books i.e. their number (19) is written in the Taurat (Torah) and the Injeel (Gospel)] and the believers may increase in Faith (as this Qur'an is the truth) and that no doubts may be left for the people of the Scripture and the believers, and that those in whose hearts is a disease (of hypocrisy) and the disbelievers may say: "What Allah intends by this (curious) example?" Thus Allah leads astray whom He wills and guides whom He wills. And none can know the hosts of your Lord but He. And this (Hell) is nothing else than a (warning) reminder to mankind.

16:2

He sends down the angels with inspiration of His Command to whom of His slaves He pleases (saying): "Warn mankind that *La ilaha illa Ana* (none has the right to be worshipped but I), so fear Me (by abstaining from sins and evil deeds)."

42:5

Nearly the heavens might be rent asunder from above them (by His Majesty), and the angels glorify the praises of their Lord, and ask for forgiveness for those on the earth, verily, Allah is the Oft-Forgiving, the Most Merciful.

25:25

And (remember) the Day when the heaven shall be rent asunder with clouds, and the angels will be sent down, with a grand descending.

35:1

All the praises and thanks be to Allah, the (only) Originator [or the (only) Creator] of the heavens and the earth, Who made the angels messengers with wings,—two or three or four. He increases in creation what He wills. Verily, Allah is Able to do all things.

Perspective:

The Greek term *angelos* literally means "messenger," so it is a common understanding among Jews and Christians that heavenly angels are divine messengers sent from the throne of God either to glorify His name on earth, to bring revelation to human beings, to strengthen them spiritually, or to fight against evil forces oppressing them. Jesus adds an eschatological function: at the end of this present age, they will cull out from God's Kingdom "everything that causes sin and all who do evil" (Matthew 13:41) consigning them to hell. Conversely, they will also gather the elect from the ends of the earth and bring them into God's presence.

According to the Quran, some angels serve to watch and record all that human beings do. Others bring revelation (Jibril [Gabriel]) so as to warn mankind; others still fight on the side of the Muslims, guard heaven or hell, etc. In 74:30–31, nineteen angels are guardians and keepers of hell; this number (apparently) agrees with what God has previously revealed to Jews and Christians, so that its inclusion here should convince them of the truth of the Quran. According to 42:5, angels glorify God in praise and ask forgiveness for human beings. On the Day of Judgment, angels will be sent out from heaven with the proclamation of God's impending decision upon each human's eternal destiny.

38. Does God permit retribution ("an eye for an eye")?

The Bible says:

Matthew 5:38–42 (ESV)
You have heard that it was said, "An eye for an eye and a tooth for a tooth." But I say to you, Do not resist the one who is evil. But if anyone slaps you on the right cheek, turn to him the other also. And if anyone would sue you and take your tunic, let him have your cloak as well. And if anyone forces you to go one mile, go with him two miles. Give to the one who begs from you, and do not refuse the one who would borrow from you.

Luke 23:34 (ESV)
Jesus said, "Father, forgive them, for they know not what they do." And they cast lots to divide his garments.

The Quran says:

2:178, 194
O you who believe! *Al-Qisas* (the Law of Equality in punishment) is prescribed for you in case of murder: the free for the free, the slave for the slave, and the female for the female. But if the killer is forgiven by the brother (or the relatives, etc.) of the killed against blood money, then adhering to it with fairness and payment of the blood money, to the heir should be made in fairness. This is an alleviation and a mercy from your Lord. So after this whoever transgresses the limits (i.e. kills the killer after taking the blood money), he shall have a painful torment. . . .

The sacred month is for the sacred month, and for the prohibited things, there is the Law of Equality (Qisas). Then whoever transgresses the prohibition against you, you transgress likewise against him. And fear Allah, and know that Allah is with *Al-Muttaqun* (the pious—see V.2:2).

5:45
And We ordained therein for them: "Life for life, eye for eye, nose for nose, ear for ear, tooth for tooth, and wounds equal for equal." But if anyone remits the retaliation by way of charity, it shall be for him an expiation. And whosoever does not judge by that which Allah has revealed, such are the Zalimun (polytheists and wrong-doers—of a lesser degree).

Perspective:

Though the Old Testament allows the law of an eye for an eye as a means of preventing the escalation of injury in the often heated acts of retaliation (i.e., *only* an eye for an eye), Jesus prohibits His followers from such an approach. Instead, He commands a law of love which demands self-restraint and the willingness to bear unjust injury rather than to seek retribution. In common Western culture this has become known as "turning the other cheek," in reference to Jesus' teaching in Matthew 5:39. Jesus Himself demonstrated this approach when on the cross He asked His Father to forgive His executioners rather than seeking their judgment.

5:45 of the Quran speaks specifically of the Old Testament law of retaliation, referred to in 2:178 as the law of equality (*qisas*). That Muhammad endorsed this approach is seen in 5:48 where Allah declares that the revelation sent down to Muhammad was given to confirm the Scripture that came before it. In the case of murder, death is prescribed for the assailant. But if the brother (or next nearest family member if there is no living brother) does not wish to pursue the penalty of death, then the guilty party (or those acting on his/her behalf) must pay blood money to the legal heir as atonement.

In this matter of the *lex talionis* (law of retaliation), we see how Muhammad aligns himself perfectly with the Jewish law, seeking the result of raw justice, whereas Jesus speaks of a higher law, one that reflects a heart of mercy and grace.

39. What should be our attitude to earthly power and glory?

The Bible says:

Luke 9:23–25 (NKJV)

He said to them all, "If anyone desires to come after Me, let him deny himself, and take up his cross daily, and follow Me. For whoever desires to save his life will lose it, but whoever loses his life for My sake will save it. For what profit is it to a man if he gains the whole world, and is himself destroyed or lost?"

Mark 9:33–37 (NKJV)

Then He came to Capernaum. And when He was in the house He asked them, "What was it you disputed among yourselves on the road?" But they kept silent, for on the road they had disputed among themselves who would be the greatest. And He sat down, called the twelve, and said to them, "If anyone desires to be first, he shall be last of all and servant of all." Then He took a little child and set him in the midst of them. And when He had taken him in His arms, He said to them, "Whoever receives one of these little children in My name receives Me; and whoever receives Me, receives not Me but Him who sent Me."

Luke 10:17–20 (NKJV)

Then the seventy returned with joy, saying, "Lord, even the demons are subject to us in Your name."

And He said to them, "I saw Satan fall like lightning from heaven. Behold, I give you the authority to trample on serpents and scorpions, and over all the power of the enemy, and nothing shall by any means hurt you. Nevertheless do not rejoice in this, that the spirits are subject to you, but rather rejoice because your names are written in heaven."

The Quran says:

8:60, 65–66

And make ready against them all you can of power, including steeds of war to threaten the enemy of Allah and your enemy, and others besides whom, you may not know but whom Allah does know. And whatever you shall spend in the Cause of Allah shall be repaid unto you, and you shall not be treated unjustly. . . .

O Prophet (Muhammad)! Urge the believers to fight. If there are twenty steadfast persons amongst you, they will overcome two hundred, and if there be a hundred steadfast persons they will overcome a thousand of those who disbelieve, because they (the disbelievers) are people who do not understand. Now Allah has lightened your (task), for He knows that there is weakness in you. So if there are of you a hundred steadfast persons, they shall overcome two hundred, and if there are a thousand of you, they shall overcome two thousand with the Leave of Allah. And Allah is with *As-Sabirin* (the patient ones, etc.).

4:36–38, 66–68

Worship Allah and join none with Him in worship, and do good to parents, kinsfolk, orphans, *Al-Masakin* (the poor), the neighbour who is near of kin, the neighbour who is a stranger, the companion by your side, the wayfarer (you meet), and those (slaves) whom your right hands possess. Verily, Allah does not like such as are proud and boastful; Those who are miserly and enjoin miserliness on other men and hide what Allah has bestowed upon them of His Bounties. And We have prepared for the disbelievers a disgraceful torment. And (also) those who spend of their substance to be seen of men, and believe not in Allah and the Last Day [they are the friends of *Shaitan* (Satan)], and whoever takes *Shaitan* (Satan) as an intimate; then what a dreadful intimate he has! ...

And if We had ordered them (saying), "Kill yourselves (i.e. the innocent ones kill the guilty ones) or leave your homes," very few of them would have done it; but if they had done what they were told, it would have been better for them, and would have strengthened their (Faith); And indeed We should then have bestowed upon them a great reward from Ourselves. And indeed We should have guided them to a Straight Way.

Perspective:

Jesus exalts servanthood, humility and self-abnegation in the service of God's Kingdom as the greatest of virtues. Those who seek the rewards of this world will inevitably miss out on the rewards of the Kingdom. Instead, the wise will deny themselves, take up their crosses (i.e., be willing to have their former lives and passions crucified) and follow Jesus. According to Kingdom ethics, the greatest of us is the one who serves the least of us. Power, even power over evil, is not to be valued as much as pursuit of intimacy with God.

The Quran enjoins worship of Allah and doing good to family, neighbors and those in need—these are the highest of priorities. Those who are miserly or who use money ostentatiously to draw attention to themselves are headed for destruction. Complete obedience to Allah, even to the point of death, is greatly rewarded by God. Earthly power is to be accrued and used only in the service of advancing Islam by force or the threat of it. Muslims are promised (8:65–66) ability in battle beyond their numbers, either twofold or tenfold, depending on Allah's will.

40. How are we to treat those in need?

The Bible says:

Luke 10:30–37 (NLT)

Jesus replied with a story: "A Jewish man was traveling from Jerusalem down to Jericho, and he was attacked by bandits. They stripped him of his clothes, beat him up, and left him half dead beside the road.

"By chance a priest came along. But when he saw the man lying there, he crossed to the other side of the road and passed him by. A Temple assistant walked over and looked at him lying there, but he also passed by on the other side.

"Then a despised Samaritan came along, and when he saw the man, he felt compassion for him. Going over to him, the Samaritan soothed his wounds with olive oil and wine and bandaged them. Then he put the man on his own donkey and took him to an inn, where he took care of him. The next day he handed the innkeeper two silver coins, telling him, 'Take care of this man. If his bill runs higher than this, I'll pay you the next time I'm here.'

"Now which of these three would you say was a neighbor to the man who was attacked by bandits?" Jesus asked.

The man replied, "The one who showed him mercy."

Then Jesus said, "Yes, now go and do the same."

The Quran says:

2:83

And (remember) when We took a covenant from the Children of Israel, (saying): Worship none but Allah (Alone) and be dutiful and good to parents, and to kindred, and to orphans and *Al-Masakin* (the poor), and speak good to people [i.e. enjoin righteousness and forbid evil, and say the truth about Muhammad Peace be upon him], and perform *As-Salat* (*Iqamat-as-Salat*), and give *Zakat*. Then you slid back, except a few of you, while you are backsliders.

9:60

As-Sadaqat (here it means *Zakat*) are only for the *Fuqara'* (poor), and *Al-Masakin* (the poor) and those employed to collect (the funds); and for to attract the hearts of those who have been inclined (towards Islam); and to free the captives; and for those in debt; and for Allah's Cause (i.e. for *Mujahidun*—those fighting in the holy wars), and for the wayfarer (a traveller who is cut off from everything); a duty imposed by Allah. And Allah is All-Knower, All-Wise.

Perspective:

Jesus' overarching teaching of love (the Golden Rule [Matthew 7:12]; "love your neighbor as yourself" [Luke 10:27]; "love your enemies" [Matthew 5:44]) reflects the Old Testament ethic that God's people are to show special care for those in need. In a parable that has come to be known as "the Good Samaritan," Jesus portrays the practical nature of love—doing whatever it takes to deal with the real needs of whoever might be in our path. Love of neighbor is measured in terms of acts of mercy.

The Quran again hearkens back to the Old Testament covenant between God and Israel, highlighting the people's responsibility to honor parents and family, and to do good to the poor, particularly in the obligatory payment of *zakat* (alms for the poor). This is enjoined on every Muslim. How one treats the poor is a measure of one's righteousness or lack thereof.

41. Why is idol worship so offensive to God?

The Bible says:

Matthew 6:24 (NIV)

No one can serve two masters. Either you will hate the one and love the other, or you will be devoted to the one and despise the other. You cannot serve both God and money.

Matthew 21:12–13 (NIV)

Jesus entered the temple courts and drove out all who were buying and selling there. He overturned the tables of the money changers and the benches of those selling doves. "It is written," he said to them, "'My house will be called a house of prayer,' but you are making it 'a den of robbers.'"

Luke 18:18–25 (NIV)

A certain ruler asked him, "Good teacher, what must I do to inherit eternal life?"

"Why do you call me good?" Jesus answered. "No one is good—except God alone. You know the commandments: 'You shall not commit adultery, you shall not murder, you shall not steal, you shall not give false testimony, honor your father and mother.'"

"All these I have kept since I was a boy," he said.

When Jesus heard this, he said to him, "You still lack one thing. Sell everything you have and give to the poor, and you will have treasure in heaven. Then come, follow me."

When he heard this, he became very sad, because he was very wealthy. Jesus looked at him and said, "How hard it is for the rich to enter the kingdom of God! Indeed, it is easier for a camel to go through the eye of a needle than for someone who is rich to enter the kingdom of God."

The Quran says:

5:60, 90

Say (O Muhammad to the people of the Scripture): "Shall I inform you of something worse than that, regarding the recompense from Allah: those (Jews) who incurred the Curse of Allah and His Wrath, those of whom (some) He transformed into monkeys and swines, those who worshipped *Taghut* (false deities); such are worse in rank (on the Day of Resurrection in the Hell-fire), and far more astray from the Right Path (in the life of this world)." ...

O you who believe! Intoxicants (all kinds of alcoholic drinks), gambling, *Al-Ansab*, and *Al-Azlam* (arrows for seeking luck or decision) are an abomination of *Shaitan's* (Satan) handiwork. So avoid (strictly all) that (abomination) in order that you may be successful.

4:48

Verily, Allah forgives not that partners should be set up with him in worship, but He forgives except that (anything else) to whom He pleases, and whoever sets up partners with Allah in worship, he has indeed invented a tremendous sin.

9:5, 28

Then when the Sacred Months (the 1st, 7th, 11th, and 12th months of the Islamic calendar) have passed, then kill the *Mushrikun* (see V.2:105) wherever you find them, and capture them and besiege them, and prepare for them each and every ambush. But if they repent and perform *As-Salat* (*Iqamat-as-Salat*), and give *Zakat*, then leave their way free. Verily, Allah is Oft-Forgiving, Most Merciful. . . .

O you who believe (in Allah's Oneness and in His Messenger (Muhammad)! Verily, the *Mushrikun* (polytheists, pagans, idolaters, disbelievers in the Oneness of Allah, and in the Message of Muhammad) are *Najasun* (impure). So let them not come near *Al-Masjid-al-Haram* (at Makkah) after this year, and if you fear poverty, Allah will enrich you if He will, out of His Bounty. Surely, Allah is All-Knowing, All-Wise.

Perspective:

Human beings were created for relationship with God, to glorify Him by finding our full delight in Him. Idols turn our hearts away from God to something lesser. Ultimately, by taking the place of God in our lives, they lead to our destruction. As Jesus makes clear in the Sermon on the Mount, no one can serve two masters. God is jealous of our commitment, and will brook no rivals. Our hearts likewise cannot entertain more than one master, no matter how hard we try to straddle the fence. When Jesus cleanses the Temple, He rails against those who in the name of serving God are really advancing their own monetary or power interests.

When we seek to find our ultimate value in something other than God, we demean His rightful glory, about which He is justly most passionate. Deep-seated idols, such as wealth, are not easily unseated from the throne of our hearts. Hence, Jesus declares, "How hard it is for the rich to enter the Kingdom of God" (Mark 10:23). Anything that comes between us and God proves deeply offensive to Him, as it should to us as well.

The worst sin, according to the Quran, is *shirk* (lit. "association"), taking anything in the creation and ascribing to it equality with God. This is the essence of idolatry. In 5:60, Allah reveals that some past idolatrous Jews were transformed into apes and pigs by divine punishment, a foretaste of their status in hell among the worst of sinners. Allah may forgive any other sin, but never that of ascribing partners to God and offering them worship along with Him. Idolaters are impure, and so are not allowed near the holy sites of Mecca, according to 9:28. All who reject the ultimate sovereignty of Allah alone will suffer the torments of hell eternally.

42. How central is mercy to God and His nature?

The Bible says:

Luke 6:32–36 (ESV)

If you love those who love you, what benefit is that to you? For even sinners love those who love them. And if you do good to those who do good to you, what benefit is that to you? For even sinners do the same. And if you lend to those from whom you expect to receive, what credit is that to you? Even sinners lend to sinners, to get back the same amount. But love your enemies, and do good, and lend, expecting nothing in return, and your reward will be great, and you will be sons of the Most High, for he is kind to the ungrateful and the evil. Be merciful, even as your Father is merciful.

Matthew 5:44–46 (ESV)

But I say to you, Love your enemies and pray for those who persecute you, so that you may be sons of your Father who is in heaven. For he makes his sun rise on the evil and on the good, and sends rain on the just and on the unjust. For if you love those who love you, what reward do you have? Do not even the tax collectors do the same?

Luke 15:3–7 (ESV)

He told them this parable: "What man of you, having a hundred sheep, if he has lost one of them, does not leave the ninety-nine in the open country, and go after the one that is lost, until he finds it? And when he has found it, he lays it on his shoulders, rejoicing. And when he comes home, he calls together his friends and his neighbors, saying to them, 'Rejoice with me, for I have found my sheep that was lost.' Just so, I tell you, there will be more joy in heaven over one sinner who repents than over ninety-nine righteous persons who need no repentance."

The Quran says:

3:129

And to Allah belongs all that is in the heavens and all that is in the earth. He forgives whom He wills, and punishes whom He wills. And Allah is Oft-Forgiving, Most Merciful.

8:70

O Prophet! Say to the captives that are in your hands: "If Allah knows any good in your hearts, He will give you something better than what has been taken from you, and He will forgive you, and Allah is Oft-Forgiving, Most Merciful."

2:284

To Allah belongs all that is in the heavens and all that is on the earth, and whether you disclose what is in your ownselves or conceal it, Allah will call you to account for it. Then He forgives whom He wills and punishes whom He wills. And Allah is Able to do all things.

2:163
And your *Ilah* (God) is One *Ilah* (God—Allah), *La ilaha illa Huwa* (there is none who has the right to be worshipped but He), the Most Beneficent, the Most Merciful.

Perspective:

Why would heaven rejoice more over the repentance of one sinner than over the righteousness of ninety-nine who need no repentance? According to Jesus, it is because mercy is the crowning attribute of God's character. Forgiveness of sins demonstrates the sacrificial, giving nature of God's heart which the just rewarding of the self-made righteous could never do (should there ever in reality be such a person). Thus, Jesus teaches His followers that as children of their heavenly Father they must learn the attribute of mercy, the capacity to love and extend goodness even to the ungrateful and wicked without expecting anything in return. This capacity sets apart those who belong to God from those who live from their own natural tendencies.

One of the most frequent descriptors of Allah in the Quran is "most merciful." He is able to forgive sins however He chooses. Yet He also punishes whomever He wills. Muhammad promises forgiveness to those taken captive in his successful battles, provided "Allah knows any good in [their] hearts" (8:70). As sovereign, God will call all human beings to account for their lives. Apparently all will be found guilty. But "then He forgives whom He will and punishes whom He will" (2:284). The impression given by the various texts of the Quran on this subject is that God's forgiveness of an individual will be based on the relative goodness of that person or upon God's sovereign decision independent of any outside influences—in essence, God's whim. The Quran provides no evidence that God prefers mercy over retribution, or vice versa.

43. What kind of sacrifice does God demand of us?

The Bible says:

Luke 14:25–33 (NLT)

A large crowd was following Jesus. He turned around and said to them, "If you want to be my disciple, you must hate everyone else by comparison—your father and mother, wife and children, brothers and sisters—yes, even your own life. Otherwise, you cannot be my disciple. And if you do not carry your own cross and follow me, you cannot be my disciple.

"But don't begin until you count the cost. For who would begin construction of a building without first calculating the cost to see if there is enough money to finish it? Otherwise, you might complete only the foundation before running out of money, and then everyone would laugh at you. They would say, 'There's the person who started that building and couldn't afford to finish it!'

"Or what king would go to war against another king without first sitting down with his counselors to discuss whether his army of 10,000 could defeat the 20,000 soldiers marching against him? And if he can't, he will send a delegation to discuss terms of peace while the enemy is still far away. So you cannot become my disciple without giving up everything you own."

Matthew 16:24–26 (NLT)

Jesus said to his disciples, "If any of you wants to be my follower, you must turn from your selfish ways, take up your cross, and follow me. If you try to hang on to your life, you will lose it. But if you give up your life for my sake, you will save it. And what do you benefit if you gain the whole world but lose your own soul? Is anything worth more than your soul?"

The Quran says:

6:162–163

Say (O Muhammad): "Verily, my *Salat* (prayer), my sacrifice, my living, and my dying are for Allah, the Lord of the 'Alamin (mankind, jinns and all that exists). He has no partner. And of this I have been commanded, and I am the first of the Muslims."

108:1–2

Verily, We have granted you (O Muhammad) *Al-Kauthar* (a river in Paradise); Therefore turn in prayer to your Lord and sacrifice (to Him only).

33:35

Verily, the Muslims (those who submit to Allah in Islam) men and women, the believers men and women (who believe in Islamic Monotheism), the men and the women who are obedient (to Allah), the men and women who are truthful (in their speech and deeds), the men and the women who are patient (in performing all the duties which Allah has ordered and in abstaining from all that Allah has forbidden), the men and the women who are humble (before their Lord

Allah), the men and the women who give *Sadaqat* (i.e. *Zakat*, and alms, etc.), the men and the women who observe *Saum* (fast) (the obligatory fasting during the month of Ramadan, and the optional *Nawafil* fasting), the men and the women who guard their chastity (from illegal sexual acts) and the men and the women who remember Allah much with their hearts and tongues (while sitting, standing, lying, etc. for more than 300 times extra over the remembrance of Allah during the five compulsory congregational prayers) or praying extra additional *Nawafil* prayers of night in the last part of night, etc.) Allah has prepared for them forgiveness and a great reward (i.e. Paradise).

4:125
And who can be better in religion than one who submits his face (himself) to Allah (i.e. follows Allah's Religion of Islamic Monotheism); and he is a *Muhsin* (a good-doer—see V.2:112). And follows the religion of Ibrahim (Abraham) *Hanifa* (Islamic Monotheism—to worship none but Allah Alone). And Allah did take Ibrahim (Abraham) as a *Khalil* (an intimate friend).

Perspective:

The disciples of Jesus were convinced that He had been sent to the world by God, and that to follow Him was to obey God. To follow Him, however, meant to surrender their lives fully to Him, subordinating all other claims on their lives so as to give Him first allegiance. Jesus speaks of this sacrifice as "tak[ing] up their cross" (Matthew 16:24) i.e., accepting the death of their old way of life in order to pursue God's will fully for their future. While this might seem too demanding, Jesus tells would-be followers that they should count the cost before becoming His disciples. He is convinced that what they give up to follow Him cannot compare with what they will gain in what He alone can offer them.

For Muhammad, there is no one who pleases God more than he who submits himself fully to God. To do this is to follow the religion of Abraham, to offer one's prayers, one's life and one's death for the Creator of all that is. Such a life entails the obedience of truth, patience, humility, generosity, obligatory prayers and fasting, sexual fidelity and regular remembrance of God. Such obedience is to be given to Allah alone. It will recognize with gratitude the role of Muhammad as the final prophet of God, through whom the believer has come to know what sacrifice Allah requires of every human being.

44. How did Jesus and Muhammad understand their calling from God?

The Bible says:

Luke 4:16–21 (NKJV)

So He came to Nazareth, where He had been brought up. And as His custom was, He went into the synagogue on the Sabbath day, and stood up to read. And He was handed the book of the prophet Isaiah. And when He had opened the book, He found the place where it was written: "The Spirit of the Lord is upon Me, because He has anointed Me to preach the gospel to the poor; He has sent Me to heal the brokenhearted, to proclaim liberty to the captives and recovery of sight to the blind, to set at liberty those who are oppressed; to proclaim the acceptable year of the Lord."

Then He closed the book, and gave it back to the attendant and sat down. And the eyes of all who were in the synagogue were fixed on Him. And He began to say to them, "Today this Scripture is fulfilled in your hearing."

John 17:1–5 (NKJV)

Jesus spoke these words, lifted up His eyes to heaven, and said: "Father, the hour has come. Glorify Your Son, that Your Son also may glorify You, as You have given Him authority over all flesh, that He should give eternal life to as many as You have given Him. And this is eternal life, that they may know You, the only true God, and Jesus Christ whom You have sent. I have glorified You on the earth. I have finished the work which You have given Me to do. And now, O Father, glorify Me together with Yourself, with the glory which I had with You before the world was."

The Quran says:

33:21, 40, 45–47

Indeed in the Messenger of Allah (Muhammad) you have a good example to follow for him who hopes in (the Meeting with) Allah and the Last Day and remembers Allah much. . . .

Muhammad is not the father of any man among you, but he is the Messenger of Allah and the last (end) of the Prophets. And Allah is Ever All-Aware of everything. . . .

O Prophet (Muhammad)! Verily, We have sent you as witness, and a bearer of glad tidings, and a warner, And as one who invites to Allah [Islamic Monotheism, i.e. to worship none but Allah (Alone)] by His Leave, and as a lamp spreading light (through your instructions from the Qur'an and the *Sunnah the legal ways of the Prophet*). And announce to the believers (in the Oneness of Allah and in His Messenger Muhammad) the glad tidings, that they will have from Allah a Great Bounty.

Perspective:

Jesus understood Himself to be God's only begotten Son, sent into the world to bring eternal life to all whom God would draw to Him. He is the Messiah predicted in the Hebrew Scriptures upon whom the Spirit was poured so that He could carry out His ministry of salvation (as foretold by Isaiah). As a result of glorifying God by accomplishing His self-offering on the cross, His Father in turn has glorified Him in heaven with the fullness of glory He originally relinquished when He became incarnate as a human being.

Muhammad saw his calling to be a witness to the one true God, a warner of those worshipping idols, and a bearer of good tidings to those who became his followers. According to the Quran, he was not only a prophet in the lineage of all the biblical leaders but the final prophet God would send into the world. He is the messenger of Allah who invites all who hear him to bow their lives in submission to God. His life stands as the paragon for which all human beings should strive.

45. What titles did Jesus and Muhammad accept for themselves?

The Bible says:

Matthew 7:22–23 (NIV)
Many will say to me on that day, "Lord, Lord, did we not prophesy in your name and in your name drive out demons and in your name perform many miracles?" Then I will tell them plainly, "I never knew you. Away from me, you evildoers!"

John 13:13 (NIV)
You call me "Teacher" and "Lord," and rightly so, for that is what I am.

Mark 14:61–62 (NIV)
Jesus remained silent and gave no answer. Again the high priest asked him, "Are you the Messiah, the Son of the Blessed One?"

"I am," said Jesus. "And you will see the Son of Man sitting at the right hand of the Mighty One and coming on the clouds of heaven."

Revelation 1:16–17 (NIV)
In his right hand he held seven stars, and coming out of his mouth was a sharp, double-edged sword. His face was like the sun shining in all its brilliance. When I saw him, I fell at his feet as though dead. Then he placed his right hand on me and said: "Do not be afraid. I am the First and the Last."

John 8:12 (NIV)
When Jesus spoke again to the people, he said, "I am the light of the world. Whoever follows me will never walk in darkness, but will have the light of life."

(See also John 10:7, 11; 14:6; 15:1.)

The Quran says:

17:93
. . . Say (O Muhammad): "Glorified (and Exalted) be my Lord (Allah) above all that evil they (polytheists) associate with Him! Am I anything but a man, sent as a Messenger?"

11:2
(Saying) worship none but Allah. Verily, I (Muhammad) am unto you from Him a warner and a bringer of glad tidings.

7:158
Say (O Muhammad): "O mankind! Verily, I am sent to you all as the Messenger of Allah—to Whom belongs the dominion of the heavens and the earth. *La ilaha illa Huwa* (none has the right to be worshipped but He); It is He Who gives life and causes death. So believe in Allah and His Messenger (Muhammad), the Prophet who can neither read nor write (i.e. Muhammad)

who believes in Allah and His Words [(this Qur'an), the Taurat (Torah) and the Injeel (Gospel) and also Allah's Word: "Be!"—and he was, i.e. "'Isa (Jesus) son of Maryam (Mary),], and follow him so that you may be guided."

5:19
O people of the Scripture (Jews and Christians)! Now has come to you Our Messenger (Muhammad) making (things) clear unto you, after a break in (the series of) Messengers, lest you say: "There came unto us no bringer of glad tidings and no warner." But now has come unto you a bringer of glad tidings and a warner. And Allah is Able to do all things.

Perspective:

During His earthly ministry, Jesus' preferred self-designation was "Son of Man," a messianic title taken from Old Testament prophetic references. Yet He also spoke of Himself as Son of God, Messiah, Lord, Teacher, and the "I Am," God's personal name revealed first to Moses. In the Gospel of John, Jesus uses seven metaphors to describe Himself in relation to the mission of salvation for which the Father sent Him into the world: "Bread of life" (6:35), "Light of the world" (8:12), "gate" for the sheepfold (10:9), "good Shepherd" (10:11), "the resurrection and the life" (11:25), "the way and the truth and the life" (14:6), "the true vine" (15:1). When Thomas exclaimed, "My Lord and my God!" upon seeing the resurrected Jesus speaking to him (John 20:28), Jesus did not reject these titles as others did when falsely accorded divine status. Instead, He demonstrated to His followers why such titles were appropriate for Him alone.

Muhammad is regularly referred to in the Quran as "only a man," like all other prophets Allah has sent into the world. Yet he is "the Messenger of Allah," i.e., the final and most authoritative spokesman of Allah's message. As such, he is the Warner of the unrepentant, but the Bringer of good tidings to those who hear and obey the Word. He accepted the designation "unlettered," meaning that he was unable to read or write, according to Islamic tradition. Some scholars have argued that this term refers not to his being unschooled (to be a successful caravan trader, Muhammad would presumably have needed at least rudimentary reading and writing skills), but rather to his being a prophet without a holy book (like the Jews and Christians had). That is why God sent the Arab peoples a holy book through him in their own language.

46. Who or what is the fullest revelation of God?

The Bible says:

John 12:44–46 (ESV)
Jesus cried out and said, "Whoever believes in me, believes not in me but in him who sent me. And whoever sees me sees him who sent me. I have come into the world as light, so that whoever believes in me may not remain in darkness."

John 14:9–11 (ESV)
Jesus said to him, "Have I been with you so long, and you still do not know me, Philip? Whoever has seen me has seen the Father. How can you say, 'Show us the Father'? Do you not believe that I am in the Father and the Father is in me? The words that I say to you I do not speak on my own authority, but the Father who dwells in me does his works. Believe me that I am in the Father and the Father is in me, or else believe on account of the works themselves."

Luke 24:25–27, 44 (ESV)
He said to them, "O foolish ones, and slow of heart to believe all that the prophets have spoken! Was it not necessary that the Christ should suffer these things and enter into his glory?" And beginning with Moses and all the Prophets, he interpreted to them in all the Scriptures the things concerning himself....

Then he said to them, "These are my words that I spoke to you while I was still with you, that everything written about me in the Law of Moses and the Prophets and the Psalms must be fulfilled."

The Quran says:

25:1
Blessed be He Who sent down the criterion (this Qur'an) to His slave (Muhammad) that he may be a warner to the 'Alamin (mankind and jinns).

6:155–157
And this is a blessed Book (the Qur'an) which We have sent down, so follow it and fear Allah, that you may receive mercy. Lest you (pagan Arabs) should say: "The Book was only sent down to two sects before us (the Jews and the Christians), and for our part, we were in fact unaware of what they studied." Or lest you (pagan Arabs) should say: "If only the Book had been sent down to us, we would surely have been better guided than they (Jews and Christians)." So now has come unto you a clear proof (the Qur'an) from your Lord, and a guidance and a mercy. Who then does more wrong than one who rejects the *Ayat* (proofs, evidences, verses, lessons, signs, revelations, etc.) of Allah and turns away therefrom? We shall requite those who turn away from Our *Ayat* with an evil torment, because of their turning away (from them).

42:52

And thus We have sent to you (O Muhammad) *Ruhan* (an Inspiration, and a Mercy) of Our Command. You knew not what is the Book, nor what is Faith? But We have made it (this Qur'an) a light wherewith We guide whosoever of Our slaves We will. And verily, you (O Muhammad) are indeed guiding (mankind) to the Straight Path (i.e. Allah's religion of Islamic Monotheism).

69:38–48

So I swear by whatsoever you see, And by whatsoever you see not, That this is verily the word of an honoured Messenger. It is not the word of a poet, little is that you believe! Nor is it the word of a soothsayer, little is that you remember! This is the Revelation sent down from the Lord of the *'Alamin* (mankind, jinns and all that exists). And if he (Muhammad) had forged a false saying concerning Us, We surely should have seized him by his right hand, And then certainly should have cut off his life artery, And none of you could withhold Us from (punishing) him. And verily, this Qur'an is a Reminder for the *Muttaqun* (pious).

Perspective:

It is clear from Jesus' teachings (see for example the Sermon on the Mount) that Jesus believed the Old Testament to be God's revealed, written Word. Yet it is also clear that He believed His teaching was the final authority for understanding all divine revelation that had preceded Him. According to Jesus, to believe in Him is to believe in His Father. To see Him is to see the Father. He is the living, most complete revelation of God, because He is the exact reflection of God in human form (see Hebrews 1:3). All prior revelation had as one of its primary purposes the prophetic task of announcing the Messiah's coming and His mission. Now that Jesus has come, the world is invited to see that He is the fullness of God's revelation.

Through Muhammad Allah declares that what Muhammad speaks are not his own words but the revelation of God sent down in the form of a book in the Arabic language. It is not the creation of any poet or soothsayer, but rather a divine reflection of what is in the "mother of all books" in heaven. It has been "sent down" as a clear proof, the criterion for right and wrong, a guidance and mercy for believers, a light to guide Allah's own slaves (i.e., Muslims) as He wishes. Not the work of human hands, the Quran is Allah's revelation, reminder to human beings, and an absolute truth which must not be trifled with. There is no authority greater than this final revelation to the world.

47. Does God have a Son?

The Bible says:

Matthew 3:16–17 (ESV)
When Jesus was baptized, immediately he went up from the water, and behold, the heavens were opened to him, and he saw the Spirit of God descending like a dove and coming to rest on him; and behold, a voice from heaven said, "This is my beloved Son, with whom I am well pleased."

Matthew 11:27 (ESV)
All things have been handed over to me by my Father, and no one knows the Son except the Father, and no one knows the Father except the Son and anyone to whom the Son chooses to reveal him.

Matthew 26:63–67 (ESV)
Jesus remained silent. And the high priest said to him, "I adjure you by the living God, tell us if you are the Christ, the Son of God." Jesus said to him, "You have said so. But I tell you, from now on you will see the Son of Man seated at the right hand of Power and coming on the clouds of heaven." Then the high priest tore his robes and said, "He has uttered blasphemy. What further witnesses do we need? You have now heard his blasphemy. What is your judgment?" They answered, "He deserves death." Then they spit in his face and struck him. And some slapped him.

Luke 9:34–36 (ESV)
As he was saying these things, a cloud came and overshadowed them, and they were afraid as they entered the cloud. And a voice came out of the cloud, saying, "This is my Son, my Chosen One; listen to him!" And when the voice had spoken, Jesus was found alone. And they kept silent and told no one in those days anything of what they had seen.

The Quran says:

43:81–82
Say (O Muhammad): "If the Most Beneficent (Allah) had a son (or children as you pretend), then I am the first of Allah's worshippers [who deny and refute this claim of yours (and the first to believe in Allah Alone and testify that He has no children)]." Glorified be the Lord of the heavens and the earth, the Lord of the Throne! Exalted be He from all that they ascribe (to Him).

72:3–4
And exalted be the Majesty of our Lord, He has taken neither a wife, nor a son (or offspring or children). And that the foolish among us [i.e. *Iblis* (Satan) or the polytheists amongst the jinns] used to utter against Allah that which was wrong and not right.

4:171
O people of the Scripture (Jews and Christians)! Do not exceed the limits in your religion, nor say of Allah aught but the truth. The Messiah' (Jesus), son of Maryam (Mary), was (no more

than) a Messenger of Allah and His Word, ("Be!"—and he was) which He bestowed on Maryam (Mary) and a spirit (*Ruh*) from Him; so believe in Allah and His Messengers. Say not: "Three (trinity)!" Cease! (it is) better for you. For Allah is (the only) One *Ilah* (God), Glory be to Him (Far Exalted is He) above having a son. To Him belongs all that is in the heavens and all that is in the earth. And Allah is All-Sufficient as a Disposer of affairs.

Perspective:

The divine Sonship of Jesus Christ is a truth affirmed frequently by Jesus in His teachings and claims. The Gospels also report two events where the voice of God declares from heaven, "This is my Son, whom I love/whom I have chosen" (Matthew 3:17; 17:5; Luke 9:35): His baptism and transfiguration. Jesus is proclaimed as God's only Son, but interpreters debate what exactly this title means. Is it a reference to Jesus' status as Israel's Messiah, a reference to divine adoption, or a declaration of Jesus' nature as one who is "of the same substance as the Father," i.e., divine Himself (see Hebrews 1:3; Colossians 1:19; 2:9)? Close attention to Jesus' reported words makes it clear that He understood Himself to have a unique relationship with God as His heavenly Father, that He claimed to have been at His Father's side from eternity, that all authority in heaven and on earth had been granted Him by His Father, that He had been sent from heaven and was returning to His Father's side after His crucifixion and resurrection. What stands out most uniquely from prior revelation is Jesus' teaching that through Him His followers could and should now address the God of Israel as "Father," adopted by God in and through Jesus, the only begotten Son.

Muhammad categorically denies that Allah has any offspring (though he seems to understand this according to pagan mythology, that some claim God has procreated through sexual encounters with human females to produce "semi-divine" sons and/or daughters). Concerning the claim that Jesus is the Son of God, Muhammad clearly taught that Jesus was only a man, called to be a prophet, but in no sense divine. Indeed, the Quran portrays Allah as forcefully rejecting the notion that He had ever taken a wife or fathered children—such is an enormous lie, worthy of only the devil and those who follow him.

48. Who is the "Alpha and Omega," the "First and Last"?

The Bible says:

Revelation 1:8, 17 (NIV)
"I am the Alpha and the Omega," says the Lord God, "who is, and who was, and who is to come, the Almighty." . . . When I saw him, I fell at his feet as though dead. Then he placed his right hand on me and said: "Do not be afraid. I am the First and the Last."

Revelation 21:6 (NIV)
He said to me: "It is done. I am the Alpha and the Omega, the Beginning and the End. To the thirsty I will give water without cost from the spring of the water of life."

Revelation 22:12–16 (NIV)
Look, I am coming soon! My reward is with me, and I will give to each person according to what they have done. I am the Alpha and the Omega, the First and the Last, the Beginning and the End.

Blessed are those who wash their robes, that they may have the right to the tree of life and may go through the gates into the city. Outside are the dogs, those who practice magic arts, the sexually immoral, the murderers, the idolaters and everyone who loves and practices falsehood.

I, Jesus, have sent my angel to give you this testimony for the churches. I am the Root and the Offspring of David, and the bright Morning Star.

The Quran says:

57:3
He is the First (nothing is before Him) and the Last (nothing is after Him), the Most High (nothing is above Him) and the Most Near (nothing is nearer than Him). And He is the All-Knower of every thing.

Perspective:

In the Old Testament, it is the Lord God, who was and is and is to come, who holds the title of "First and Last." In the New Testament book of Revelation, again it is the Lord God who takes this title, now in the form of "Alpha and Omega," the first and last letters of the Greek alphabet. Since the *lingua franca* of New Testament times was Greek, all the original readers of these texts would understand this claim as equivalent to "First and Last." What is so startling in the book of Revelation is that the resurrected Jesus applies these titles to Himself. "Do not be afraid," He says to John, "I am the First and the Last. I am the Living One" (1:17–18). In the closing chapters, Jesus gathers these titles together and lays claim to them: "I am the Alpha and the Omega, the Beginning and the End" (21:6); "I am the Alpha and the Omega, the First and the Last, the Beginning and the End" (22.13). Ascribing to Himself these titles reserved for God alone, Jesus lays claim to equality with God, and His followers ultimately embraced this claim, while continuing to believe that there is only one God. Over the next few centuries the church would grapple with how the Father and Jesus and the Holy Spirit could all equally be worshipped as one God—this led to what we now confess as the Trinitarian nature of God—one divine being comprised of three co-equal, co-eternal persons.

Allah alone is described as "the First and the Last" in Sura 57:3. The phrase "Alpha and Omega" is not found in the Quran as it was written in Arabic to an Arabic-speaking audience, the vast majority of which was not familiar with the Greek alphabet and so would not understand the allusion. Since in Islamic thought only God exists from eternity to eternity, the descriptor "First and Last" can only justly be applied to Him. As the context of this verse makes clear, all else that exists was created by Allah, and so could not predate Him. Likewise, all creation is subject to His judgment, existing only at His pleasure, and so remains contingent. Nothing in the universe can rightfully claim to be "the Last," since only God has the quality of aseity.

49. Are the Jews God's chosen people?

The Bible says:

Matthew 10:5–8 (NLT)

Jesus sent out the twelve apostles with these instructions: "Don't go to the Gentiles or the Samaritans, but only to the people of Israel—God's lost sheep. Go and announce to them that the Kingdom of Heaven is near. Heal the sick, raise the dead, cure those with leprosy, and cast out demons. Give as freely as you have received!"

Matthew 23:37–39 (NLT)

O Jerusalem, Jerusalem, the city that kills the prophets and stones God's messengers! How often I have wanted to gather your children together as a hen protects her chicks beneath her wings, but you wouldn't let me. And now, look, your house is abandoned and desolate. For I tell you this, you will never see me again until you say, "Blessings on the one who comes in the name of the LORD!"

Luke 19:9–10 (NLT)

Jesus responded, "Salvation has come to this home today, for this man has shown himself to be a true son of Abraham. For the Son of Man came to seek and save those who are lost."

John 4:22 (NLT)

You Samaritans know very little about the one you worship, while we Jews know all about him, for salvation comes through the Jews.

The Quran says:

45:16

And indeed We gave the Children of Israel the Scripture, and the understanding of the Scripture and its laws, and the Prophethood; and provided them with good things, and preferred them above the 'Alamin (the world).

5:18, 51, 82

And the Jews and the Christians say: "We are the children of Allah and His loved ones." Say: "Why then does He punish you for your sins?" Nay, you are but human beings, of those He has created, He forgives whom He wills and He punishes whom He wills.

O you who believe! Take not the Jews and the Christians as *Auliya'* (friends, protectors, helpers, etc.), they are but *Auliya'* to one another.

Verily, you will find the strongest among men in enmity to the believers (Muslims) the Jews and those who are *Al-Mushrikun*, and you will find the nearest in love to the believers those who say: "We are Christians." That is because amongst them are priests and monks, and they are not proud.

9:30

And the Jews say: 'Uzair (Ezra) is the son of Allah, and the Christians say: Messiah is the son of Allah ... Allah's Curse be on them, how they are deluded away from the truth!

Perspective:

Jesus understood Himself to have been sent first to "the lost sheep of Israel" (Matthew 15:24) and He confines His ministry principally to the Jews during His earthly ministry. As Messiah He is the fulfillment of God's promises made to Abraham and his descendants. Yet God's promise to Abraham was inclusive of the larger world: "I will make you into a great nation, and I will bless you . . . and all peoples on earth will be blessed through you" (Genesis 12:2–3). Jesus' relatively few encounters with Gentiles in need demonstrate this inclusive grace, serving as a foretaste of the Great Commission (Matthew 28:19–20) where He commands His followers to make disciples of all nations. For Jesus, the Jews remain the chosen people, not as the exclusive recipients of God's love but as the nation through whom God's salvation has come to the world in the person and work of Jesus the Messiah. As He said to the Samaritan woman, "Salvation is *from* the Jews" (John 4:22, emphasis added). How important it is to pay attention to prepositions: *from* the Jews, *for* all people (Jews and Gentiles).

In the Quran, the stature of the Jews as God's chosen people of the past ("chosen above the rest of the world") is highlighted, usually as an indictment of how far they have fallen from God's will by the time of Muhammad. They received God's Scripture, the ability to understand it, the prophets who continually proclaimed it and the blessing of material prosperity from the hand of Allah. But they are no longer the chosen, for they have (with few exceptions) rejected the teachings of Muhammad, increasing instead "in obstinate rebellion and disbelief." Therefore Allah has "put enmity and hatred among them till the Day of Resurrection" (5:64). Who are those most antagonistic to Muslims? According to 5:82 it is the Jews and all idolaters. As a result, Muslims are called to do battle against all people, including Jews and Christians, upon whom is Allah's curse, until they are subdued and willingly live under Islamic rule. In rejecting the claims of Muhammad, the Jews "prove" that they are no longer the chosen of God.

50. What does true worship of God entail?

The Bible says:

Matthew 4:8–10 (NKJV)
Again, the devil took Him up on an exceedingly high mountain, and showed Him all the kingdoms of the world and their glory. And he said to Him, "All these things I will give You if You will fall down and worship me."

Then Jesus said to him, "Away with you, Satan! For it is written, 'You shall worship the LORD your God, and Him only you shall serve.'"

John 4:21, 23–24 (NKJV)
Jesus said to her, "Woman, believe Me, the hour is coming when you will neither on this mountain, nor in Jerusalem, worship the Father.... But the hour is coming, and now is, when the true worshipers will worship the Father in spirit and truth; for the Father is seeking such to worship Him. God is Spirit, and those who worship Him must worship in spirit and truth."

Mark 12:28–30 (NKJV)
Then one of the scribes came, and ... asked Him, "Which is the first commandment of all?"

Jesus answered him, "The first of all the commandments is: 'Hear, O Israel, the LORD our God, the LORD is one. And you shall love the LORD your God with all your heart, with all your soul, with all your mind, and with all your strength.' This is the first commandment."

The Quran says:

2:125, 150
And (remember) when We made the House (the Ka'bah at Makkah) a place of resort for mankind and a place of safety. And take you (people) the *Maqam* (place) of Ibrahim (Abraham) as a place of prayer, and We commanded Ibrahim (Abraham) and Isma'il (Ishmael) that they should purify My House (the Ka'bah at Makkah) for those who are circumambulating it, or staying (*I'tikaf*), or bowing or prostrating themselves (there, in prayer)....

And from wheresoever you start forth (for prayers), turn your face in the direction of *Al-Masjid-al-Haram* (at Makkah), and wheresoever you are, turn your faces towards, it (when you pray) so that men may have no argument against you except those of them that are wrongdoers, so fear them not, but fear Me!—And so that I may complete My Blessings on you and that you may be guided.

4:43
O you who believe! Approach not *As-Salat* (the prayer) when you are in a drunken state until you know (the meaning) of what you utter, nor when you are in a state of *Janaba*, (i.e. in a state of sexual impurity and have not yet taken a bath) except when travelling on the road (without enough water, or just passing through a mosque), till you wash your whole body. And if you are

ill, or on a journey, or one of you comes after answering the call of nature, or you have been in contact with women and you find no water, perform *Tayammum* with clean earth and rub therewith your faces and hands....

5:6

O you who believe! When you intend to offer *As-Salat* (the prayer), wash your faces and your hands (forearms) up to the elbows, rub your heads, and (wash) your feet up to ankles...

62:9

O you who believe (Muslims)! When the call is proclaimed for the *Salat* (prayer) on the day of Friday, come to the remembrance of Allah and leave off business (and every other thing), that is better for you if you did but know!

Perspective:

To love God with all we have to offer is at the heart of true worship, according to Jesus. God is to have no rivals for our affection or for our attentiveness. Hence, as Jesus says to the Samaritan woman in John 4, the worship that God seeks from human beings is a matter of spirit and truth. That is, worship is to be authentic as an expression of who we really are before God, not something done merely as a ritual or as an external act from which our hearts are disconnected. Further, worship is to be based on what God has revealed of His nature and works on behalf of the world, such that our response to Him is based on truth, not our imaginations or wishes.

Unlike Jesus, who taught that true worship is not limited to certain holy sites, Muhammad claims that the holy sites of Mecca are the place Muslims are to offer their worship to Allah. If unable to be physically present there, they are to face toward Mecca as they offer their ritual prayers and devotion. Acceptable worship demands that the believer is in the right state of mind (i.e., not impaired by alcohol or other drugs), ritually clean (having washed after sexual contact, illness, returning from a journey, or having just gone to the bathroom). All other matters of life are to be laid aside when the call to prayer issues from the mosque, especially for the Friday noon prayers, when all Muslim men are expected to attend together. Allah warns that His blessings are contingent upon adherents following the laws laid out in the Quran for prayer.

51. What is God's central message to humanity?

The Bible says:

Mark 1:14–15 (NKJV)

Now after John was put in prison, Jesus came to Galilee, preaching the gospel of the kingdom of God, and saying, "The time is fulfilled, and the kingdom of God is at hand. Repent, and believe in the gospel."

John 3:3–8 (NKJV)

Jesus answered and said to him, "Most assuredly, I say to you, unless one is born again, he cannot see the kingdom of God."

Nicodemus said to Him, "How can a man be born when he is old? Can he enter a second time into his mother's womb and be born?"

Jesus answered, "Most assuredly, I say to you, unless one is born of water and the Spirit, he cannot enter the kingdom of God. That which is born of the flesh is flesh, and that which is born of the Spirit is spirit. Do not marvel that I said to you, 'You must be born again.' The wind blows where it wishes, and you hear the sound of it, but cannot tell where it comes from and where it goes. So is everyone who is born of the Spirit."

John 6:28–29 (NKJV)

Then they said to Him, "What shall we do, that we may work the works of God?"

Jesus answered and said to them, "This is the work of God, that you believe in Him whom He sent."

The Quran says:

5:3

Forbidden to you (for food) are: *Al-Maytatah* (the dead animals), blood, the flesh of swine, and the meat of that which has been slaughtered as a sacrifice for others than Allah, or has been slaughtered for idols, etc., or on which Allah's Name has not been mentioned while slaughtering, and that which has been killed by strangling, or by a violent blow, or by a headlong fall, or by the goring of horns—and that which has been (partly) eaten by a wild animal—unless you are able to slaughter it (before its death)—and that which is sacrificed (slaughtered) on *An-Nusub* (stone altars). (Forbidden) also is to use arrows seeking luck or decision, (all) that is *Fisqun* (disobedience of Allah and sin). This day, those who disbelieved have given up all hope of your religion, so fear them not, but fear Me. This day, I have perfected your religion for you, completed My Favour upon you, and have chosen for you Islam as your religion. But as for him who is forced by severe hunger, with no inclination to sin (such can eat these above-mentioned meats), then surely, Allah is Oft-Forgiving, Most Merciful.

22:77–78

O you who believe! Bow down, and prostrate yourselves, and worship your Lord and do good that you may be successful. And strive hard in Allah's Cause as you ought to strive. He has chosen you), and has not laid upon you in religion any hardship, it is the religion of your father Ibrahim. It is He (Allah) Who has named you Muslims both before and in this (the Qur'an), that the Messenger (Muhammad) may be a witness over you and you be witnesses over mankind! So perform *As-Salat*, give *Zakat* and hold fast to Allah. He is your *Maula* (Patron, Lord, etc.), what an Excellent *Maula* and what an Excellent Helper!

33:35
Verily, the Muslims…, the men and the women who are obedient (to Allah), the men and women who are truthful, the men and the women who are patient, the men and the women who are humble, the men and the women who give *Sadaqat* (i.e. *Zakat*, and alms, etc.), the men and the women who observe *Saum* (fasting), the men and the women who guard their chastity (from illegal sexual acts) and the men and the women who remember Allah much with their hearts and tongues Allah has prepared for them forgiveness and a great reward (i.e. Paradise).

Perspective:

Jesus proclaims that through His incarnational ministry the Kingdom of God has drawn near, the powers of darkness are being rolled back from their domination of creation, and human beings everywhere are welcomed into relationship with God as children who may benefit from His healing, rescuing work, both now and through eternity. This message is good news because the offer is freely given. All that is required to participate in the Kingdom of God is to repent—to turn away from one's former way of life and to turn toward God and His will instead. This happens as the Spirit of God transforms a person's heart (he becomes "born again"—John 3:3), which is evidenced by his or her desire now to put his or her trust in Jesus, the one whom the Father has sent as Savior to the world.

Muhammad maintained that his message was the same as all prophets before him: that there is no God but Allah, so that nothing has the right to be worshiped except Him alone. Those who submit to Allah will be guided in the straight path (the way of Islam); if they carry out the duties God enjoins and avoid the actions He proscribes, He will bless them with the potential reward of paradise. If they fail to obey, they will likely suffer the same fate as those who refuse to submit to Allah: the flames of hell. God will serve as the judge of all; His sovereign judgments, whatever they may be toward any individual, are final and determinative.

52. Does God predestine people to heaven or hell?

The Bible says:

John 6:64–65 (NIV)

"Yet there are some of you who do not believe." For Jesus had known from the beginning which of them did not believe and who would betray him. He went on to say, "This is why I told you that no one can come to me unless the Father has enabled them."

John 10:26–28 (NIV)

You do not believe because you are not my sheep. My sheep listen to my voice; I know them, and they follow me. I give them eternal life, and they shall never perish; no one will snatch them out of my hand.

Matthew 22:1–14 (NIV)

The kingdom of heaven is like a king who prepared a wedding banquet for his son. He sent his servants to those who had been invited to the banquet to tell them to come, but they refused to come.

Then he sent some more servants and said, "Tell those who have been invited that I have prepared my dinner: My oxen and fattened cattle have been butchered, and everything is ready. Come to the wedding banquet."

But they paid no attention and went off—one to his field, another to his business. The rest seized his servants, mistreated them and killed them. The king was enraged. He sent his army and destroyed those murderers and burned their city.

Then he said to his servants, "The wedding banquet is ready, but those I invited did not deserve to come. So go to the street corners and invite to the banquet anyone you find." So the servants went out into the streets and gathered all the people they could find, the bad as well as the good, and the wedding hall was filled with guests.

But when the king came in to see the guests, he noticed a man there who was not wearing wedding clothes. He asked, "How did you get in here without wedding clothes, friend?" The man was speechless.

Then the king told the attendants, "Tie him hand and foot, and throw him outside, into the darkness, where there will be weeping and gnashing of teeth."

For many are invited, but few are chosen.

The Quran says:

6:125

And whomsoever Allah wills to guide, He opens his breast to Islam, and whomsoever He wills to send astray, He makes his breast closed and constricted, as if he is climbing up to the sky. Thus Allah puts the wrath on those who believe not.

7:179

And surely, We have created many of the jinns and mankind for Hell. . . .

9:51

Say: "Nothing shall ever happen to us except what Allah has ordained for us. He is our *Maula* (Lord, Helper and Protector)." And in Allah let the believers put their trust.

76:29–30

Verily! This is an admonition, so whosoever wills, let him take a Path to his Lord. But you cannot will, unless Allah wills.

Perspective:

The net is cast widely by Jesus as He offers salvation to any and all willing to respond to His message: "Come to me, all you who are weary and burdened, and I will give you rest" (Matthew 11:28). Yet in the immediate context of this offer, Jesus declares that the Father has blinded the arrogant to Kingdom truths, and that no one knows the Father except those to whom the Son chooses to reveal Him.

In a complementary passage (John 10:22–29), Jesus declares that no one can turn to Jesus in faith unless the Father grants him the capacity. Likewise, He explains to those who refuse to believe in Him that the reason they don't believe is that they are not His sheep. If they were sheep of God's fold, they would recognize the Shepherd's voice and follow Him. But they do not believe because they are not God's sheep. Westerners tend to turn Jesus' words around, thinking that it is the choice to believe which qualifies one to belong to God—"You are not my sheep because you do not believe." But Jesus reverses the causation. The choice as to whether we belong to God or not rests in God's initiative, not our will. "We choose because He first chose us," would be an appropriate paraphrase.

The Quran implies a presumption of human freedom to embrace or reject Muhammad's message (cf. 18:29). But 76:29–31 undercuts this apparent freedom by declaring that whatever a human wills, he cannot will except as Allah determines. And Allah's determination to heaven or hell rests upon nothing except His private whim or decision. He forgives or punishes as He wills. Those who become Muslims do so because Allah has willed to open their hearts; those who end up in hell have been led astray by Allah's determination to close their hearts to His message. In 7:179 Allah openly declares that He has "created many of the jinn and mankind for hell," accomplishing this by causing them to stray from His commands. This eternal predestination is part of a larger, overarching fatalism that informs much of the Quran: "Nothing shall ever happen to us except what Allah has ordained for us" (9:51).

53. Whom did God send to the world to guide believers after Jesus' ascension?

The Bible says:

John 14:15–17, 25–26 (ESV)

If you love me, you will keep my commandments. And I will ask the Father, and he will give you another Helper, to be with you forever, even the Spirit of truth, whom the world cannot receive, because it neither sees him nor knows him. You know him, for he dwells with you and will be in you. . . . These things I have spoken to you while I am still with you. But the Helper, the Holy Spirit, whom the Father will send in my name, he will teach you all things and bring to your remembrance all that I have said to you.

John 15:26 (ESV)

When the Helper comes, whom I will send to you from the Father, the Spirit of truth, who proceeds from the Father, he will bear witness about me.

John 16:7–14 (ESV)

Nevertheless, I tell you the truth: it is to your advantage that I go away, for if I do not go away, the Helper will not come to you. But if I go, I will send him to you. And when he comes, he will convict the world concerning sin and righteousness and judgment: concerning sin, because they do not believe in me; concerning righteousness, because I go to the Father, and you will see me no longer; concerning judgment, because the ruler of this world is judged.

I still have many things to say to you, but you cannot bear them now. When the Spirit of truth comes, he will guide you into all the truth, for he will not speak on his own authority, but whatever he hears he will speak, and he will declare to you the things that are to come. He will glorify me, for he will take what is mine and declare it to you.

The Quran says:

61:6

And (remember) when 'Isa (Jesus), son of Maryam (Mary), said: "O Children of Israel! I am the Messenger of Allah unto you confirming the Taurat [(Torah) which came] before me, and giving glad tidings of a Messenger to come after me, whose name shall be Ahmed. But when he (Ahmed i.e. Muhammad) came to them with clear proofs, they said: "This is plain magic."

Perspective:

In His final teaching of the disciples before His crucifixion, Jesus promises them that after He is taken from them and returns to the Father they will be given "another Advocate" (Paraclete) to be with them forever. Jesus names this Advocate—"the Spirit of truth" (John 14:17). He bears the same nature as Jesus, their first Advocate. The Spirit is another Advocate of the same type as Jesus. He will carry on with them the ministry that Jesus inaugurated, teaching them all things and reminding them of Jesus' words. He will testify about Jesus to the disciples, i.e., will always point them toward Him and the significance of His life, death, resurrection, ascension and second coming. The Spirit's goal is to glorify Jesus in the disciples and in the world, by convicting hearts and manifesting God's victory over the prince of this world. In John 14:26, this Advocate is identified clearly as the Holy Spirit, known to all Christians as the third member of the Trinity.

Only one verse in the Quran plants the idea that Jesus predicted the coming of a messenger after His own death. In 61:6 Jesus gives "glad tidings of a Messenger to come after me, whose name shall be Ahmad." The names Muhammad and Ahmad derive from the same root (h-m-d), and so are variations on the idea of praise. Muhammad means "the praised one"; Ahmad means "more praiseworthy." In searching through Jesus' teachings in the Gospels, Muslims discovered no clear prophecy about Muhammad, but have settled on Jesus' teaching regarding the Paraclete as pointing to Muhammad.

The Greek term *parakletos* does not mean "praised one," but a similar sounding one, *periklutos*, does mean "praised one." Though there is no textual evidence at all supporting this claim, Muslims commonly argue that Jesus really said *periklutos* not *parakletos*, and hence was prophesying about Muhammad's future ministry, not about the Holy Spirit. Aside from the lack of any evidence for this in ancient manuscripts, there is the fact that Jesus makes repeated references to the individual in question as the Spirit of truth or the Holy Spirit, and reassures the disciples that the Spirit will be with them soon after Jesus is taken away. Since Muhammad was not born until A.D. 570, Muslims must argue either that Jesus was not a very accurate prophet or that everything else He is credited with saying about the Advocate/Praised One was actually a corruption of what He really taught, which was apparently then lost to history until Muhammad began his ministry and declared that Jesus prophesied his coming.

54. Was Jesus executed by crucifixion?

The Bible says:

Luke 23:38–46 (NLT)
A sign was fastened above him with these words: "This is the King of the Jews."

One of the criminals hanging beside him scoffed, "So you're the Messiah, are you? Prove it by saving yourself—and us, too, while you're at it!"

But the other criminal protested, "Don't you fear God even when you have been sentenced to die? We deserve to die for our crimes, but this man hasn't done anything wrong." Then he said, "Jesus, remember me when you come into your Kingdom."

And Jesus replied, "I assure you, today you will be with me in paradise."

By this time it was about noon, and darkness fell across the whole land until three o'clock. The light from the sun was gone. And suddenly, the curtain in the sanctuary of the Temple was torn down the middle. Then Jesus shouted, "Father, I entrust my spirit into your hands!" And with those words he breathed his last.

Matthew 20:17–19 (NLT)
As Jesus was going up to Jerusalem, he took the twelve disciples aside privately and told them what was going to happen to him. "Listen," he said, "we're going up to Jerusalem, where the Son of Man will be betrayed to the leading priests and the teachers of religious law. They will sentence him to die. Then they will hand him over to the Romans to be mocked, flogged with a whip, and crucified. But on the third day he will be raised from the dead."

Matthew 26:2 (NLT)
As you know, Passover begins in two days, and the Son of Man will be handed over to be crucified.

The Quran says:

4:157–159
And because of their saying (in boast), "We killed Messiah 'Isa (Jesus), son of Maryam (Mary), the Messenger of Allah,"—but they killed him not, nor crucified him, but the resemblance of 'Isa (Jesus) was put over another man (and they killed that man), and those who differ therein are full of doubts. They have no (certain) knowledge, they follow nothing but conjecture. For surely; they killed him not [i.e. 'Isa (Jesus), son of Maryam (Mary)]: But Allah raised him ['Isa (Jesus)] up (with his body and soul) unto Himself (and he is in the heavens). And Allah is Ever All-Powerful, All-Wise. And there is none of the people of the Scripture (Jews and Christians), but must believe in him ['Isa (Jesus), son of Maryam (Mary), as only a Messenger of Allah and a human being], before his ['Isa (Jesus) or a Jew's or a Christian's] death (at the time of the appearance of the angel of death). And on the Day of Resurrection, he ['Isa (Jesus)] will be a witness against them.

Perspective:

Each of the Gospels records with great detail the event of Jesus' crucifixion by Roman authorities, as well as the fact that His lifeless body was taken from the cross after release by the executioners and entombed in a burial site provided by a wealthy disciple named Joseph of Arimathea, after he had secured permission from Pontius Pilate, the Roman prefect of Judea. Jesus Himself had predicted His death by crucifixion a number of times in the presence of His disciples. There is no question that the Gospels speak with one voice on the question of the manner of Jesus' death—He suffered the fate reserved by the Roman Empire for its worst criminals: crucifixion.

Only one text in the Quran deals specifically with the question of Jesus' death, and the most perspicacious reading of it clearly denies that Jesus was crucified. It portrays the Jews as boasting that they had killed the Messiah (which, of course, no Jew would boast about), but then denies that the Jews had indeed carried out this action—it only appeared to them that they had. Instead, as Islamic tradition has it, they crucified someone they thought was Jesus, but Jesus Himself was rescued by Allah and taken to heaven without having suffered death of any sort, much less crucifixion. He will return to earth before the end of history to live out the remainder of His life as leader of the Islamic community, will die of natural causes and be buried in Medina next to Muhammad's tomb. Following this, the Day of Reckoning will begin.

55. Was Jesus raised from the dead?

The Bible says:

Matthew 26:31–32 (NLT)
On the way, Jesus told them, "Tonight all of you will desert me. For the Scriptures say, 'God will strike the Shepherd, and the sheep of the flock will be scattered.' But after I have been raised from the dead, I will go ahead of you to Galilee and meet you there."

Luke 24:36–39, 45–46 (NLT)
Just as they were telling about it, Jesus himself was suddenly standing there among them. "Peace be with you," he said. But the whole group was startled and frightened, thinking they were seeing a ghost!

"Why are you frightened?" he asked. "Why are your hearts filled with doubt? Look at my hands. Look at my feet. You can see that it's really me. Touch me and make sure that I am not a ghost, because ghosts don't have bodies, as you see that I do." . . .

Then he opened their minds to understand the Scriptures. And he said, "Yes, it was written long ago that the Messiah would suffer and die and rise from the dead on the third day."

John 20:24–29 (NLT)
One of the twelve disciples, Thomas (nicknamed the Twin), was not with the others when Jesus came. They told him, "We have seen the Lord!"

But he replied, "I won't believe it unless I see the nail wounds in his hands, put my fingers into them, and place my hand into the wound in his side."

Eight days later the disciples were together again, and this time Thomas was with them. The doors were locked; but suddenly, as before, Jesus was standing among them. "Peace be with you," he said. Then he said to Thomas, "Put your finger here, and look at my hands. Put your hand into the wound in my side. Don't be faithless any longer. Believe!"

"My Lord and my God!" Thomas exclaimed.

Then Jesus told him, "You believe because you have seen me. Blessed are those who believe without seeing me."

The Quran says:

3:55
And (remember) when Allah said: "O 'Isa (Jesus)! I will take you and raise you to Myself and clear you [of the forged statement that 'Isa (Jesus) is Allah's son] of those who disbelieve, and I will make those who follow you (Monotheists, who worship none but Allah) superior to those who disbelieve [in the Oneness of Allah, or disbelieve in some of His Messengers, e.g. Muhammad , 'Isa (Jesus), Musa (Moses), etc., or in His Holy Books, e.g. the Taurat (Torah),

the Injeel (Gospel), the Qur'an] till the Day of Resurrection. Then you will return to Me and I will judge between you in the matters in which you used to dispute."

19:33–34
And *Salam* (peace) be upon me the day I was born, and the day I die, and the day I shall be raised alive!" Such is 'Isa (Jesus), son of Maryam (Mary). (it is) a statement of truth, about which they doubt (or dispute).

Perspective:

Jesus predicts not only His death by crucifixion but also His resurrection from the grave. The resurrection accounts show a fearful and doubting response from the disciples when the risen Lord appears in their midst. Jesus demonstrates to them the tangibility of His presence by taking food from them to eat, allowing them to touch His body, particularly the scars of His crucifixion, and by conversing with them over a wide range of topics. Yet He is able to appear and disappear at will and shows full awareness of what has transpired in the lives of the disciples between the times of His physical appearances in their midst. It is in Jesus' post-resurrection meetings with the disciples that they are commissioned to take the message of the gospel of salvation to the ends of the earth, making disciples for the Kingdom of God from every tribe and tongue and people and nation. The resurrection of Jesus Christ is the assurance and impetus for the announcement of the gospel to the world.

Since the Quran is interpreted by orthodox Muslims to declare that Jesus was never executed by crucifixion (see question 54), it cannot subsequently declare that Jesus has been resurrected from the dead. However, there are two curious passages in the Quran, one which declares God's intention to raise Jesus to Himself in order to foil the attempts of those who sought Jesus' life (3:55), and the other a blessing pronounced by Jesus upon Himself which indicates the logical progression of life, death and resurrection. Nowhere in this text is there any hint that Allah would raise Jesus to heaven prior to His death only to send Him back to earth just prior to the Day of Reckoning to live out the remainder of His natural life, then die, and then be resurrected with all other human beings. Thus, Muhammad seemed to have believed that Jesus has not yet been resurrected because He has not yet died. But He has been "raptured" in the sense of having been taken up alive to heaven, awaiting His future return to live out His remaining years of natural life before dying, after which He will be resurrected.

56. What constitutes blasphemy before God?

The Bible says:

Luke 12:10 (NKJV)

And anyone who speaks a word against the Son of Man, it will be forgiven him; but to him who blasphemes against the Holy Spirit, it will not be forgiven.

Matthew 5:33–37 (NKJV)

Again you have heard that it was said to those of old, "You shall not swear falsely, but shall perform your oaths to the Lord." But I say to you, do not swear at all: neither by heaven, for it is God's throne; nor by the earth, for it is His footstool; nor by Jerusalem, for it is the city of the great King. Nor shall you swear by your head, because you cannot make one hair white or black. But let your "Yes" be "Yes," and your "No," "No." For whatever is more than these is from the evil one.

Mark 7:20–23 (NKJV)

He said, "What comes out of a man, that defiles a man. For from within, out of the heart of men, proceed evil thoughts, adulteries, fornications, murders, thefts, covetousness, wickedness, deceit, lewdness, an evil eye, blasphemy, pride, foolishness. All these evil things come from within and defile a man."

The Quran says:

5:72–73

Surely, they have disbelieved who say: "Allah is the Messiah ['Isa (Jesus)], son of Maryam (Mary)." But the Messiah ['Isa (Jesus)] said: "O Children of Israel! Worship Allah, my Lord and your Lord." Verily, whosoever sets up partners in worship with Allah, then Allah has forbidden Paradise for him, and the Fire will be his abode. And for the *Zalimun* (polytheists and wrong-doers) there are no helpers. Surely, disbelievers are those who said: "Allah is the third of the three (in a Trinity)." But there is no *ilah* (god) but One *Ilah* (God). And if they cease not from what they say, verily, a painful torment will befall the disbelievers among them.

9:30

And the Jews say: 'Uzair (Ezra) is the son of Allah, and the Christians say: Messiah is the son of Allah. That is a saying from their mouths. They imitate the saying of the disbelievers of old. Allah's Curse be on them, how they are deluded away from the truth!

7:180

And (all) the Most Beautiful Names belong to Allah, so call on Him by them, and leave the company of those who belie or deny (or utter impious speech against) His Names. They will be requited for what they used to do.

Perspective:

The Greek term from which we get our English word *blasphemy* means literally "speech that harms." In the Bible it principally refers to language or actions which demean the glory of God by belittling His divine attributes or by ascribing them to someone/something other than God. In the Gospels, Jesus is accused of blasphemy by Jewish antagonists who understand His claims by word or action to be declarations of equality with God (see Matthew 12:12–32). Jesus Himself addresses the sin of blasphemy in teaching about oath-taking (not demeaning God by taking His name in vain) as well as by speaking of "blasphemy against the Spirit" (12:31; see question 22). Essentially, to blaspheme the Holy Spirit is to attribute to the devil the divine revelation and actions of the Spirit as expressed in and through Jesus. It is the complete upending of truth and morality, where good is spoken of as evil, and evil as good.

The principal cause of blasphemy in the Quran is the sin of *shirk*, which literally translates as "association." Thus when a person attributes God's unique attributes and/or stature to something created, and in essence makes that equal with God, that individual has committed blasphemy. Muslims, as a result, agree with Jesus' Jewish opponents in the charge that if Jesus was claiming equality with God in having the authority to forgive sins and to call God Father, and to claim eternal existence, etc., then He was guilty of blasphemy because, they assume, He was only human. Another piece of evidence in the Quran of blasphemy against God is the obstinate unwillingness to accept Muhammad as God's prophet and his words as God's revelation. To dismiss Muhammad and the Quran is to demean God's ultimacy and to reject His authority, thus impugning His glory by committing blasphemy.

57. Why did God send all prior prophets into the world?

The Bible says:

Matthew 5:17 (ESV)
Do not think that I have come to abolish the Law or the Prophets; I have not come to abolish them but to fulfill them.

Matthew 26:55–56 (ESV)
At that hour Jesus said to the crowds, "Have you come out as against a robber, with swords and clubs to capture me? Day after day I sat in the temple teaching, and you did not seize me. But all this has taken place that the Scriptures of the prophets might be fulfilled." Then all the disciples left him and fled.

Luke 18:31 (ESV)
Taking the twelve, he said to them, "See, we are going up to Jerusalem, and everything that is written about the Son of Man by the prophets will be accomplished."

Luke 24:25–27, 44 (ESV)
He said to them, "O foolish ones, and slow of heart to believe all that the prophets have spoken! Was it not necessary that the Christ should suffer these things and enter into his glory?" And beginning with Moses and all the Prophets, he interpreted to them in all the Scriptures the things concerning himself. . . .

Then he said to them, "These are my words that I spoke to you while I was still with you, that everything written about me in the Law of Moses and the Prophets and the Psalms must be fulfilled."

John 1:45 (ESV)
Philip found Nathanael and said to him, "We have found him of whom Moses in the Law and also the prophets wrote, Jesus of Nazareth, the son of Joseph."

The Quran says:

6:48, 130
And We send not the Messengers but as givers of glad tidings and as warners. So whosoever believes and does righteous good deeds, upon such shall come no fear, nor shall they grieve. . . .

O you assembly of jinns and mankind! "Did not there come to you Messengers from amongst you, reciting unto you My Verses and warning you of the meeting of this Day of yours?" . . .

2:213, 285
Mankind were one community and Allah sent Prophets with glad tidings and warnings, and with them He sent the Scripture in truth to judge between people in matters wherein they differed. . . .

The Messenger (Muhammad) believes in what has been sent down to him from his Lord, and (so do) the believers. Each one believes in Allah, His Angels, His Books, and His Messengers. They say, "We make no distinction between one another of His Messengers"—and they say, "We hear, and we obey. (We seek) Your Forgiveness, our Lord, and to You is the return (of all)."

14:4
And We sent not a Messenger except with the language of his people, in order that he might make (the Message) clear for them. Then Allah misleads whom He wills and guides whom He wills. And He is the All-Mighty, the All-Wise.

Perspective:

God's primary purpose in sending prophets before Jesus was to prepare His people for the coming of Jesus. This He accomplished by shaping their moral and spiritual vision through the Law as well as by prophetic revelation of God's ultimate goal of sending His Son into the world as the Suffering Servant who would sacrifice His life as a perfect atonement for the sins of the human race. Jesus claimed He had come to fulfill the Law and the Prophets, that the course of His life and ministry had been predicted by the Old Testament prophets, that the primary intent of the Scriptures revealed by God through the prophets was to point to the Messiah and to prepare people to follow Him. The fact that Jesus alluded often to this is evidence that He saw His ministry as the capstone to all God had promised the world through His previous revelations.

Muhammad believed that God has sent all prior prophets to the world with the same basic message that he himself proclaimed to the Arab peoples. Each prophet (or messenger) had been equipped to share the good news with his own people in their own native language, that if they believed in the only true God and obeyed His laws, God would favor them on the Day of Judgment, and to warn them that if they rejected God or disobeyed His laws, they would suffer eternal torment in hell. This is the distilled message of Islam. Thus, Muslims believe that the message they have received from Muhammad is the same message that Moses delivered to his people and that Jesus delivered to His listeners. Any claim that Jesus was more than a messenger, that He came not to warn people but to save them by His atoning sacrifice, is categorically rejected by Muhammad and his followers. Muhammad's primary distinction from all other prophets is, according to the Quran, that he is the last in the line of God's prophets, so his words are of universal import and have foremost authority.

58. Is Jesus the Messiah?

The Bible says:

John 4:25–26 (NIV)

The woman said, "I know that Messiah" (called Christ) "is coming. When he comes, he will explain everything to us."

Then Jesus declared, "I, the one speaking to you—I am he."

John 17:3 (NIV)

Now this is eternal life: that they know you, the only true God, and Jesus Christ, whom you have sent.

Matthew 16:13–17, 20 (NIV)

When Jesus came to the region of Caesarea Philippi, he asked his disciples, "Who do people say the Son of Man is?"

They replied, "Some say John the Baptist; others say Elijah; and still others, Jeremiah or one of the prophets."

"But what about you?" he asked. "Who do you say I am?"

Simon Peter answered, "You are the Messiah, the Son of the living God."

Jesus replied, "Blessed are you, Simon son of Jonah, for this was not revealed to you by flesh and blood, but by my Father in heaven. . . ." Then he ordered his disciples not to tell anyone that he was the Messiah.

Matthew 24:4–5 (NIV)

Jesus answered: "Watch out that no one deceives you. For many will come in my name, claiming, 'I am the Messiah,' and will deceive many."

The Quran says:

3:45

(Remember) when the angels said: "O Maryam (Mary)! Verily, Allah gives you the glad tidings of a Word from Him, his name will be the Messiah 'Isa (Jesus), the son of Maryam (Mary), held in honour in this world and in the Hereafter, and will be one of those who are near to Allah."

4:171

O people of the Scripture (Jews and Christians)! Do not exceed the limits in your religion, nor say of Allah aught but the truth. The Messiah 'Isa (Jesus), son of Maryam (Mary), was (no more than) a Messenger of Allah and His Word, which He bestowed on Maryam (Mary) and a spirit (*Ruh*) from Him; so believe in Allah and His Messengers. Say not: "Three (trinity)!" Cease! (it is) better for you. For Allah is (the only) One *Ilah* (God), Glory be to Him (Far Exalted is He) above having a son. To Him belongs all that is in the heavens and all that is in the earth. And Allah is All-Sufficient as a Disposer of affairs.

5:72, 75

Surely, they have disbelieved who say: "Allah is the Messiah ['Isa (Jesus)], son of Maryam (Mary)." But the Messiah ['Isa (Jesus)] said: "O Children of Israel! Worship Allah, my Lord and your Lord." Verily, whosoever sets up partners in worship with Allah, then Allah has forbidden Paradise for him, and the Fire will be his abode . And for the *Zalimun* (polytheists and wrong-doers) there are no helpers....

The Messiah ['Isa (Jesus)], son of Maryam (Mary), was no more than a Messenger; many were the Messengers that passed away before him. His mother [Maryam (Mary)] was a *Siddiqah* [i.e. she believed in the words of Allah and His Books].

Perspective:

The term *Messiah* or its Greek transliterated form *Christ* literally means "anointed one". In the Jewish thought of Jesus' day, the Messiah was the yearned-for leader to be sent by God to lead the nation of Israel to sovereign independence and then to dominion over the world. He would be Israel's spiritual as well as military and kingly leader, uniquely anointed by God with His Spirit to proclaim and usher in the Kingdom of heaven. The Gospels are littered with claims by Jesus Himself as well as by His followers that He is that promised and expected Messiah. So clearly is Jesus understood to be Messiah by His followers that the title becomes essentially an appendage to His name from the time of the New Testament onward: Jesus Christ.

The Quran speaks eleven times of "the Messiah" (*al-Masih*). Without exception, these are all references to Jesus, and the term seems honorific. It is doubtful that Muhammad would have used this unique title of Jesus had he been aware of its meaning in Jewish and Christian thought. Elsewhere Muhammad emphasizes against Christian claims that though Jesus is both Messiah and prophet, He is only a human, as are all other prophets. Muslims who are troubled by the Quran's usage of the term *Messiah* for Jesus sometimes argue that since the term means literally "anointed one" and Jesus must have been anointed by God to be a true prophet, there is nothing untoward with this term being used about Him. All prophets have been anointed by God. This is certainly true in a generic way. Yet the term as used is specific ("the Anointed One"), not general ("an anointed one"). The fact is, the term *Messiah* is used only of Jesus in the Quran, not of any of the other twenty-eight or so prophets named in its pages, including Muhammad himself. In sum, the Quran declares Jesus to be the Messiah, though it never defines what is meant by that term.

59. Who has the power to resurrect the dead to eternal life?

The Bible says:

John 6:39–40, 44 (NIV)

This is the will of him who sent me, that I shall lose none of all those he has given me, but raise them up at the last day. For my Father's will is that everyone who looks to the Son and believes in him shall have eternal life, and I will raise them up at the last day. . . .

No one can come to me unless the Father who sent me draws them, and I will raise them up at the last day.

John 11:21–26 (NIV)

"Lord," Martha said to Jesus, "if you had been here, my brother would not have died. But I know that even now God will give you whatever you ask."

Jesus said to her, "Your brother will rise again."

Martha answered, "I know he will rise again in the resurrection at the last day."

Jesus said to her, "I am the resurrection and the life. The one who believes in me will live, even though they die; and whoever lives by believing in me will never die."

John 14:6 (NIV)

Jesus answered, "I am the way and the truth and the life. No one comes to the Father except through me."

Revelation 1:18 (NIV)

I am the Living One; I was dead, and now look, I am alive for ever and ever! And I hold the keys of death and Hades.

The Quran says:

17:49–52

And they say: "When we are bones and fragments (destroyed), should we really be resurrected (to be) a new creation?" Say (O Muhammad) "Be you stones or iron," Or some created thing that is yet greater (or harder) in your breasts." Then, they will say: "Who shall bring us back (to life)?" Say: "He Who created you first!". . .

20:55

Thereof (the earth) We created you, and into it We shall return you, and from it We shall bring you out once again.

22:6–7

That is because Allah, He is the Truth, and it is He Who gives life to the dead, and it is He Who is Able to do all things. And surely, the Hour is coming, there is no doubt about it, and certainly, Allah will resurrect those who are in the graves.

46:33

Do they not see that Allah, Who created the heavens and the earth, and was not wearied by their creation, is Able to give life to the dead? Yes, He surely is Able to do all things.

Perspective:

One of Jesus' central claims as Savior and Lord is that He has the authority and capacity to resurrect the dead to eternal life. This power is heralded by His resurrection of the dead (in raising a widow's son [Luke 7:11–17] and Lazarus [John 11] back to earthly life), but it is seen clearly in His own victory over death, His present resurrection life, His many claims and promises concerning the resurrection of the dead and His unique role as "the resurrection and the life" (John 11:25). In Jewish thought, only God can bring about resurrection, which the Pharisees of Jesus' day expected God would accomplish on the Day of Judgment. Jesus' claim to this role is an implicit claim to divinity.

Muhammad believed in and proclaimed a coming resurrection. The Quran declares that the only one who resurrects is "He who originally created you" (i.e., Allah; see 17:51). From the earth God created human beings; to the earth they return at death; and from their earthly graves God will bring them out again on the day of resurrection.

Only Allah has the inherent power to give life to the dead. In light of all this, it is amazing that the Quran records of Jesus that in His ministry he both brought to life things that were inanimate, and brought back to life (resurrected) individuals who had died. Of course, Muhammad is quick to say that Jesus could do this only with the permission of Allah; that is, He did not have this power inherently. Nevertheless, no other person in the Quran is cited as exercising this power to give life to the dead. While only Allah can resurrect in the last day, the Quran paints a tantalizing picture of Jesus that approaches that of Jesus in the New Testament before pulling back from the claim that He is the resurrection and the life, the Living One who holds the keys to death and hades.

60. Who will be the final judge of humanity?

The Bible says:

Matthew 7:21–23 (NLT)
Not everyone who calls out to me, "Lord! Lord!" will enter the Kingdom of Heaven. Only those who actually do the will of my Father in heaven will enter. On judgment day many will say to me, "Lord! Lord! We prophesied in your name and cast out demons in your name and performed many miracles in your name." But I will reply, "I never knew you. Get away from me, you who break God's laws."

Matthew 19:28 (NLT)
Jesus replied, "I assure you that when the world is made new and the Son of Man sits upon his glorious throne, you who have been my followers will also sit on twelve thrones, judging the twelve tribes of Israel."

Matthew 25:31–33 (NLT)
When the Son of Man comes in his glory, and all the angels with him, then he will sit upon his glorious throne. All the nations will be gathered in his presence, and he will separate the people as a shepherd separates the sheep from the goats. He will place the sheep at his right hand and the goats at his left.

John 5:25–29 (NLT)
And I assure you that the time is coming, indeed it's here now, when the dead will hear my voice—the voice of the Son of God. And those who listen will live. The Father has life in himself, and he has granted that same life-giving power to his Son. And he has given him authority to judge everyone because he is the Son of Man. Don't be so surprised! Indeed, the time is coming when all the dead in their graves will hear the voice of God's Son, and they will rise again. Those who have done good will rise to experience eternal life, and those who have continued in evil will rise to experience judgment.

The Quran says:

7:87
And if there is a party of you who believes in that with which I have been sent and a party who do not believe, so be patient until Allah judges between us, and He is the Best of judges."

50:29–34
The Sentence that comes from Me cannot be changed, and I am not unjust (to the least) to the slaves." On the Day when We will say to Hell: "Are you filled?" It will say: "Are there any more (to come)?" And Paradise will be brought near to the *Muttaqun* (pious) not far off. (It will be said): "This is what you were promised.... Enter you therein in peace and security; this is a Day of eternal life!"

82:18–19

Again, what will make you know what the Day of Recompense is? (It will be) the Day when no person shall have power (to do) anything for another, and the Decision, that Day, will be (wholly) with Allah.

95:8

Is not Allah the Best of judges?

Perspective:

Jesus' most frequent self-designation was "Son of Man." In the parable of the sheep and goats (Matthew 25:31–46) Jesus speaks of the Son of Man occupying the throne of judgment before which all the nations of the earth will be gathered. As King and Judge, the Son of Man will determine the eternal destiny of each individual on the basis of whether he is a "sheep" (one who recognizes and follows the Shepherd's voice) or a "goat" (one who is not part of the flock of God). The Son of Man's decree will send each person to his/her proper destiny. In other passages Jesus makes it clear that judgment is based on whether individuals have a personal relationship with Him or not, by recognizing His voice and trusting in Him, or by remaining unhearing and placing their trust in other gods. In the context of first century Judaism, where the God of Israel alone sits on the throne of judgment, Jesus' claim to rightfully rule from that throne is nothing less than stunning.

Allah is the best of judges, according to the Quran (95:8). Hence, when He issues final decrees on the Day of Recompense, no one will be able to gainsay His decisions.

Muhammad apparently was faced with deceivers who presented themselves as true Muslims but around whom there swirled much controversy about the sincerity of their allegiance. In this context his warnings that Allah is able see into the heart and will not be fooled is meant to intimidate and ward off those hypocrites who are playing the religious game in order to advance their own standing in the community. Allah's final judgment will vindicate Muhammad and his message.

About the Author

What are the odds that a son born to a Muslim father, raised for more than a decade in Saudi Arabia, schooled in western philosophy and psychology, and then trained in eastern mysticism, should become a resolute Christian and a minister of the gospel?

Mateen was the second of four children born to a Syrian Muslim who had married an American while studying at the University of Wisconsin. Some years after Mateen's birth, the family moved to Saudi Arabia where his father worked as an oil company executive. During his early teens Mateen began a search for God, largely through reading. For six years he focused on eastern mysticism and meditation including a stay at an ashram in India. Yet his nagging questions, *Who is God? How can I know Him?* remained unanswered.

God guided Mateen toward an answer to those questions by bringing him into contact with genuine Christians. He found these people by visiting a friend who attended a small Christian University in Arkansas. The love and compassion of students there impressed him so deeply that he repeatedly asked them the source. They in turn repeatedly pointed him to Christ. And he repeatedly searched for some other explanation: culture, family ties, unwritten rules of relationship. Eventually they challenged him, "Read the four gospels of the New Testament. Get to know Jesus." He took up the challenge. After days of reading, study, and prayer, at the age of twenty Mateen found salvation through Christ-and the fulfillment of his long search. As is common in Middle Eastern families, he soon paid a high cost for his newfound faith: isolation from his father for more than a decade.

By the end of his college years, Mateen sensed God's call to Christian ministry. After completing a B.A. at Stanford University, he graduated from Fuller Seminary earning M.Div. and M.A. degrees in Biblical Studies and Theology. After several years of pastoral work he returned to school earning a Ph.D. in New Testament Studies from Durham University in England.

Mateen and his wife Cindy have three children: Brittany and Strider and Kendall, who are all in their 20s.

Pastor Mateen's prior ministry includes an associate position for a small-town Presbyterian church in Wyoming, solo pastor of a young suburban church in Arizona, and Minister of Adult Education at First Presbyterian of Colorado Springs, a church of more than five thousand people. He served as senior pastor of Immanuel Presbyterian (in the Evangelical Presbyterian denomination) prior to coming to First Presbyterian, Edmond, in July 2007.

A frequent speaker about Islam, Mateen sees his experience on both sides of the Christian-Muslim divide as providing unique opportunity to create bridges of understanding. His great hope is that God will use him to reveal the love of Jesus to both sides. "God will provide direction to those who seek him and God will equip his people to do his will."